REMEMBERING MUSCLE BEACH

Just to see one person hold another in a hand-to-hand is pretty special. Here we have six holding six, a rare combination.

REMEMBERING MUSCLE BEACH

• WHERE HARD BODIES BEGAN •
PHOTOGRAPHS AND MEMORIES

BY HAROLD ZINKIN WITH BONNIE HEARN

ANGEL CITY PRESS

ANGEL CITY PRESS, INC.
PMB 880, 2118 Wilshire Boulevard
Santa Monica, California 90403
310.395.9982
www.angelcitypress.com

First published in 1999 by Angel City Press
1 3 5 7 9 10 8 6 4 2
FIRST EDITION

ISBN 1-883318-01-7

Remembering Muscle Beach
By Harold Zinkin with Bonnie Hearn
Copyright © 1999 by Harold Zinkin and Bonnie Hearn

Designed by Susan Anson and Maritta Tapanainen

LIBRARY OF CONGRESS CATALOGING-IN-PUBLICATION DATA
Zinkin, Harold, 1922-
Remembering Muscle Beach : where hard bodies began : photographs and memories
by Harold Zinkin with Bonnie Hearn. — 1st ed.
p. cm.
Includes bibliographical references.
ISBN 1-883318-01-7 (hard)
1. Bodybuilding—California—Santa Monica—History.
2. Bodybuilding—California—Santa Monica—Pictorial works.
3. Santa Monica (Calif.)—Social life and customs—Pictorial works.
I. Hearn, Bonnie, 1945-
II. Title.
GV546.5 .Z56 1999
646.7'5—dc21
99-6322
CIP

Printed in Hong Kong

In the midst of winter, I finally learned that there was in me an invincible summer. —Albert Camus

This book is dedicated to the one-time kids of Muscle Beach
and that invincible summer we continue to share—
and to the memory of John Grimek,
who inspired us all. —H.Z.

▶ **Balancing and muscle skill are demonstrated by the 1939 Mr. America Bert Goodrich, right, and partner George Redpath on the platform at Muscle Beach.**

CONTENTS

◁ Almost fifty years before the Olympic gymnasts were doing giant swings on the uneven bars, Helen Smith, shown with Moe Most, was swinging on the high bar at Muscle Beach.

PROLOGUE

"The most important thing at Muscle Beach was the friendships we made."
—Joe Gold, founder of Gold's Gym

If there's any doubt about the renown of Muscle Beach in the forties, just look at an old map of southern California: "Muscle Beach" appears in larger type than "Santa Monica."

On a recent visit to Muscle Beach in Santa Monica, I saw only one rather lonely sign. Yes, all that remains of those years between 1934 and 1958 is a pole and a plaque that reads: "The Original Location of Muscle Beach. The Birthplace of the Physical Fitness Boom of the Twentieth Century." It's not much of a monument to a time when there were as many bodies in the air as on the ground—a time when a bunch of sometimes silly, often painstaking stunts launched many careers and changed many lives.

To those of us who participated in them, those early days at Muscle Beach were giddy and exciting times. We were fine-tuning our athletic skills and forging new ground in physical fitness. Although most of the country didn't know and didn't care about the so-called physical-culture movement, the gang at Muscle Beach

◁ **We were the first four men to perform this trick, and to my knowledge, no one has ever duplicated it in the United States. I'm on the bottom in the backbend, Moe Most is standing on top of me supporting Jack LaLanne who's supporting Gene Miller, the top man. We worked months to perfect this, and the stunt became world famous.**

The main platform at Muscle Beach was just a short run to the legendary Santa Monica Pier.

proved every day that no one had to settle for the body he or she was born with. We took control of our bodies, using every muscle we could.

The Beach was an oddity then, far ahead of its time. The general public and most of the medical profession believed that working with weights was harmful to the muscles. Although most people weren't interested in bodybuilders, just about everyone liked watching the gymnasts, wrestlers and weightlifters who performed at Muscle Beach. By observing the athletes' exercise routines and their impromptu shows, people picked up the not-so-subtle message of fitness. Besides it was great free entertainment, something Americans needed in those days.

In the mid-thirties, most of the country was happy just to be working, not to mention eating on a regular basis. As children of the Depression era, my friends and I needed some relief—we wanted to play. But it wasn't always easy finding time to play since I was attending junior high and mopping the cafeteria floor after school for extra money.

My father earned fifteen dollars a week as an upholsterer for Angelus Furniture Company. Although we were poor, no one we knew had much more money than we did. It was a weekly reality to visit the Perfection Bakery by Los Angeles City Hall on Temple Street, and stand in lines a block or two long after the trucks came in. We'd offer whatever we could spare—thirty cents, fifty cents, ninety cents—and they'd fill our gunny sacks with the appropriate amount of bread that hadn't been sold that day. If we happened to get some sugar-iced "snails" with raisins, we hit the jackpot.

The bread lasted a week, and by then, you could break it with a brick. My mother would buy fish heads and cook them in a little olive oil, which she said made her questionable ingredients taste more like meat. She'd serve the concoction over the broken bread. That's what we had, and that's what our dog had. We all ate the same.

It was in those days, not bleak but far from opulent, that I first set eyes on the place that would change my life forever. Although he was two years older, my friend Abe Regenbogen was as interested in tumbling and gymnastics as I was. He thought it was a good idea to show me the Beach at Santa Monica and introduce me to some of the older guys I'd be meeting the following year at Roosevelt High School in east Los Angeles.

What a sight it was—gymnasts flying through the air, landing on a platform in the sand. According to Abe, it was fine to join in or just watch. I felt secure in my tumbling abilities, and I wanted to test myself. I also wanted to see if these Beach people might know something I didn't. My first day there blends with all of the days that followed. What I remember is that I felt like Alice stepping through the looking glass into Wonderland.

Before long I was part of the crazy bunch of kids who performed shows on the Beach. I never dreamed that in a few years I'd be doing real shows, selling bonds for the war effort. I couldn't begin to think that far ahead. All I knew was that the Beach was the best part of my life. It was the relief and release I was looking for.

Not long after I discovered the Beach, my finances improved, along with those of the rest of the nation. By 1939, I was setting pins in a bowling alley making twenty-five cents an hour. We did it by hand in those days. I had to adjust them quickly, hoping to hell the guy at the other end wasn't drunk (which he usually was) and then jump up on the three-foot-high rail before the big black ball came crashing toward me. I also worked in a theater in east L.A., putting words on the marquee, a job that required a ladder, a bunch of

▶ **George Eiferman became Mr. Philadelphia, Mr. America and Mr. Universe, and he always worked with young people, helping them to be fit. Here he poses with Beverly Jocher, Miss Muscle Beach in 1952.**

I'm in the center, with my two best friends in school, Joe Gold, left, and Bob Tucker. Taken in the late 1930s, this photo shows us at our favorite place, Muscle Beach, Santa Monica. We were inseparable.

letters and an affinity for high altitudes. With even minimal money, however, came wheels.

A bunch of us would stuff ourselves inside my Model A Ford and cram three or four in the trunk. Heads and feet sticking out, we made that twenty-mile drive from east L.A. to Santa Monica. Soto Street to Washington Boulevard to Venice Beach, Main Street and beyond. Then and now, I could drive it in my sleep.

During these early years on the Beach, our band of eager athletes spent weekends and the long days of summer working out and honing our skills in the cool breezes of the Pacific. Those I shared the sand with in the mid- to late-thirties were the true founders of Muscle Beach, the people who established its reputation and witnessed its growth as a unique contribution to physical fitness. It is their stories that I want to share with you in this book.

At Muscle Beach, Russ Saunders learned the techniques that landed him jobs in major films such as *Singing in the Rain* and *The Three Musketeers*, roles that made him one of the top stuntmen—if not *the* top stuntman—in Hollywood. And it was at Muscle Beach that I first got the idea that led to my inventing the Universal Gym Machine. (I didn't call it the Zinkin because I was afraid no one would know who I was.) It was there that Vic Tanny, the master promoter and gym entrepreneur, came up with the concept of a Mr. California contest and many other competitions that brought recognition and honor to those of us who won. And it was there that women such as Relna Brewer and Pudgy Eville Stockton proved that attractive women could and possibly should lift weights—including live, human, male weights, when they felt like it. At Muscle Beach, we learned and shared information about nutrition, with less sophistication, but with the same passion that health-conscious people of all ages discuss healthful eating today.

The Beach we visited every weekend was a magnet for fitness leaders around the world. When John Grimek (who became the first and second American Athletic Union-sanctioned Mr. America in 1940 and 1941, as well as Mr. Universe in 1948), attended the 1936 Olympic games in Berlin, the Europeans bombarded him with questions about "that beach in Santa Monica." The strength magazines were full of Muscle Beach photos. Tenor Mario Lanza visited in disguise. Jane Russell pursued her husband-to-be Bob Waterfield there. Colorful figures like wrestlers Gorgeous George, Pepper Gomez and Baron Leone mingled with the movie stars. It began as a place where a few friends could work out in the sand and grew to include a mismatched but amiable group of athletes, circus performers, wrestlers, college gymnasts, movie stunt people and just about anyone else who wanted to join. On weekends the crowd of spectators could easily top ten thousand, all lining the sidewalk to watch amazing stunts.

Jack LaLanne, a weekend visitor, was already a star to those of us who knew that this fitness-preaching, vegetarian kid wasn't a nut. At Muscle Beach, Jack was in his element, and he didn't have to worry about the many who disregarded his accomplishments. Jack and I still laugh about how we met, and of course, we each tell a slightly different version of the story. I'd heard about Jack LaLanne for a long time. I knew that he'd started a modern-day health club in 1931 in Berkeley, that he could do a thousand pushups, and that he had quite a reputation as a wrestler. Jack had also heard about me, and we were both curious about each other.

Some people shake hands when they're introduced, and some make small talk. Although Jack and I may have engaged in both of those polite gestures, I remember only what followed—a furious wrestling match in the surf and on the sand. Right away I knew I was dealing with someone who, like me, didn't have the word "quit" in his vocabulary. He claims we were at it for ten minutes, but I know it had to be closer to fifteen or twenty. When Jack says there was no winner that day, he's being kind. I was so tired I couldn't see straight. He was like a crab that just kept crawling, crawling, crawling over the wet sand. Even after all these years I wouldn't want to wrestle with him again.

I look today at a photograph taken of Jack, me and a few other fellows: from the top, Gene Miller, Jack LaLanne, Moe Most, all of them balanced on a guy doing a full backbend—me. Although many of my sixth-grade classmates had predicted that I would become a strong man in the circus, this stunt took more than

▲ Stuntman Russ Saunders with the Beach's two leading strong women, Relna Brewer, left, and Pudgy Stockton.

strength. It took us two years of practice to be able to hold that pyramid in position long enough for a photograph. I usually worked in the second position on a pyramid, but I was the understander here, and I knew we had a small margin of error in the balancing process. We'd already been practicing with Moe standing on my backbend while holding another person. Adding another body on top was the next natural step. It was the only time we ever did it. Almost fifty years later to the day, we saw a photograph of Russian acrobats doing it in an acrobatics magazine. When Paula Unger Boelsems visited Russia, she saw our photograph on the wall of a gymnasium. The pose has yet to be repeated in the United States.

I remember how, almost magically, as participants, we became as close as one body, each of us giving up any independent role we originally felt. When I look at that photograph today, I see not just our bodies, but our faces—Gene, happy and secure on top; Jack, as always, determined to meet whatever challenges life handed him. Beneath Jack stood Moe, a wonderful understander in many of the photographs you'll see in these pages. In its upside-down state, my body was stretched to its limits and my face was all smiles. Even in this exaggerated pose, I loved every minute I spent at Muscle Beach. I couldn't imagine anything I'd rather do.

All of us—from top to bottom in that photo and in the rest of the photos I'll share with you in this book—were full of hope. Maybe that's part of the reason Muscle Beach is such a source of interest for many today. That hope carried us farther than we could have guessed at the time.

Those who didn't understand what we were doing called us "Muscleheads," just as others with different abilities were called "Eggheads." Although the term stung at the time, history has proven that we were on the right track, and that

▲ **Former Mr. Universe John Grimek was the role model for Muscle Beach regulars.**

"muscle" isn't a dirty word. As you look at more than sixty years of photographs and read all the memories that go with them, you will realize that those times played a great part in the success of numerous fitness greats. More legends were shaped per square foot at Muscle Beach than anywhere else in the world.

The Beach certainly made a difference in my life. It taught me to think about fitness, to think about possibilities rather than impossibilities, about my own strengths that went beyond my muscles. In 1945, I won first place in my division at the AAU National Weightlifting Championship competition. That was on a Saturday. The next day, in the same place, the same room, I placed second in the Mr. America contest that Clarence Ross won. It was quite a weekend. I never became that strong man in the circus, but I was once dubbed the Henry Ford of Fitness. It was a title that, like being named the first Mr. California, both embarrasses and pleases me. In 1960, the first of five patents was issued for my Universal Gym Machine. Although I knew that the Universal was an essential product for schools and the military, I wasn't sure how to get it there. Between 1960 and 1963, we sold just one per month. In 1964, we sold one per week, and in 1965, we sold one unit per hour. Universal was purchased in 1968—a multi-million-dollar sale— and I continued as chief executive officer. If I'm proud of anything, it's that machine and the fact that there probably isn't one professional athlete in the world who hasn't worked out on a Universal at least once. If that machine turned me into the Henry Ford of Fitness, keep in mind that I learned to drive, metaphorically speaking, at Muscle Beach.

Muscle Beach really was glue. You became a part of it. You became a part of the activities. There wasn't anywhere else in the world where you could find that kind of life or get to know people like these.

Muhammad Ali once said, "The man who views the world the same at fifty as he did at thirty has wasted twenty years of his life." At seventy-six plus, I view that world with very different eyes today. Yet my goal here is to shut my eyes and take you back to the early days of the original Muscle Beach. It was the birthplace of the fitness movement. Indeed, it's where many hard bodies began. So many fitness greats got their starts there. But we were kids, remember? And what kids care about, Muscle Beach delivered in spades. In a word—fun. Fun—that's the way it started.

‖〜‖

CHAPTER ONE

MUSCLE BEACH EARNS ITS NAME

"It seems that everyone on the beach can stand on his hands."
—*Los Angeles Times*, 1938

A hamburger cost a dime. "Down by the River" and "Lazy Bones" blared from jukeboxes on the pier, and at what was to become Muscle Beach, Santa Monica, something was happening that would change the course of fitness in the country.

In 1934, a few young athletes, looking for a soft place to land while working out, migrated to the Santa Monica Beach Playground. About the same time, some circus and vaudeville performers independently did the same. A handstand here. A somersault there. Tricks were shared, routines created, equipment acquired or built from scratch. Muscle magazines recorded the feats of these talented people who easily posed, preened, flew, climbed, lifted and generally piled on each other's bodies. Within a few years, athletes, acrobats, college gymnasts, movie stunt people, circus performers and folks from all over the world were flocking to the Beach.

But before the crowds, before the muscle, this small stretch of beach served as a children's playground. Although confusion has long clouded the history of how

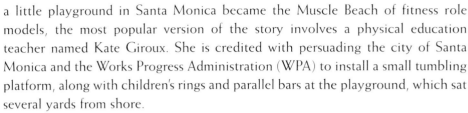

a little playground in Santa Monica became the Muscle Beach of fitness role models, the most popular version of the story involves a physical education teacher named Kate Giroux. She is credited with persuading the city of Santa Monica and the Works Progress Administration (WPA) to install a small tumbling platform, along with children's rings and parallel bars at the playground, which sat several yards from shore.

During the early thirties in an effort to put people back to work, the WPA supported federal public works programs throughout the nation. In Santa Monica, the beaches were crowded with the unemployed, and the WPA saw the efforts at the playground as dual-purpose—a way to provide work and recreation facilities.

Although Giroux and Santa Monica High School football coach Vincent Shutt were in charge of the children on the beach, they had nothing to do with the installation of the more professional adult equipment that followed. That long-overdue recognition belongs to Paul Brewer, Jimmy Pfeiffer and Al Niederman.

Brewer came from St. Louis, Missouri, in 1926, when he was nine. The Santa Monica Pier's entertainment consisted of a roller coaster and the carousel (it's still there today!), and the nearby playground had only small rings, a simple metal merry-go-round and bars about five feet high.

The Brewers moved to northern California that same year, returning to Santa Monica in 1929. Upon his return, Paul recalled, the playground hadn't changed in three years. He joined the John Adams Junior High tumbling team, and in 1931 learned arm-to-arm balancing, back flips and handstands. His school had only an elementary-school style combination horizontal bar/parallel bars/horizontal ladder in the sand pit next to the boys' locker room. The 1933 Long Beach earthquake damaged the school buildings, and the administration canceled plans for a boys' gym. As juniors in high school, Brewer and Jimmy Pfeiffer spent more and more time practicing gymnastics down at Santa Monica Beach. At its playground, they met Al Niederman, a former gymnast in his thirties, who worked as a mechanic for Santa Monica's local bus company. Niederman was the unofficial coach for their small group. He also taught Brewer's sister Relna how to do flyaway somersaults off the small rings.

Although they appreciated the soft sand for landing purposes, the young people didn't like getting it in their eyes. Brewer put a rug down in 1933. That rug, which ran north to south, was the beginning of the Muscle Beach that would grow

▷ Gordon McRae in 1939.

up around them. A canvas tarp, running east to west, followed in 1934.

In 1936, Niederman built a
ground-level wooden platform situ-
ated north and south, about three
by twelve feet in size, and one hundred fifty yards from the Pacific.
People tumbled and did twisting
somersaults off the end, into the
sand less than an inch below. They
placed the tarp on this almost-
ground-level platform, but had to
remove it because it slid during
stunts.

Brewer, Pfeiffer and Niederman
tried to get the city to upgrade the
original equipment, and received a
reluctant go-ahead, based on their
willingness to provide the labor
necessary to install it. Niederman
contributed a welding torch and
other tools, and in 1936 built the
high rings and parallel bars, doing
most of the assembly work himself.

Relna Brewer was the first
strong woman of Muscle Beach.
This photograph was taken in the
mid 1930s.

Relna Brewer McRae and
weightlifter Joe DiPietro and
Lynne McRae in 1944.

The high rings extended about twenty-five feet into the air,
allowing for high swinging and dramatic routines before an
acrobat landed on the sand. The parallel bars stood about
shoulder height and were used for regular gymnastic routines as
well as for whatever inventive and experimental positions we
could think up.

Paul Brewer wanted to be the first to perform a handstand
on those brand-new parallel bars. He went for it a little too
soon after Niederman welded the bars together, and still
remembers the burn.

And Kate Giroux? In the early thirties, one child was hurt on the metal
merry-go-round and another was injured on the swings. To help prevent further

accidents, the WPA officially hired Giroux to watch over children at the playground. She had nothing to do with the athletes who frequented the Beach. In fact, asserts Relna Brewer, Giroux went to the city, demanding, "I want you to get those crazy acrobats off my beach." She was told that no one could be forced from the beach, but she wasn't satisfied. Giroux was determined to banish the athletes. However, someone got the politic idea to include her in one of the photographs of the Muscle Beach crowd, and her attitude gradually improved. Then the children in her charge began telling and showing Giroux what they had learned from "those crazy acrobats." Since Relna, Paul and their friends were the first there, I've never doubted their story of those days. The Brewers and their friends were clearly the original Muscle Beach pioneers.

HOW THE BEACH GOT ITS NAME

Just how Muscle Beach came by its distinct moniker has been another source of entertaining stories mixing myth with reality. The most common of the incorrect theories is that the name derived from the mussels on the pilings of the Santa Monica Pier. But the Beach wasn't about shellfish; it was about people. All of the beaches in the area had their own identities, based on the crowds frequenting them. Canyon Mouth, known as State Beach, about two to three miles north of the Santa Monica Playground, was frequented by many gays. One mile south was Montana Jetty, aptly called Volleyball Beach, where many volleyball players, most of them high school students, hung out. Over time, our beach became Muscle Beach. In fact, that's all I ever remember calling it.

Certainly the muscle aspect of that primarily acrobatic beach increased by the late thirties. Those who frequented nearby beaches used to sneer in the direction of Santa Monica, saying, "That's where the muscles are." It was not a compliment in those days, but it wasn't an evaluation of the local sea creatures either.

Relna Brewer recalls playing at the Beach under a big sign that read "Santa Monica Beach Playground."

◀ **Jim and Kay Starkey had a professional balancing act.**

◀ **A couple of ring dismounts have the makings of a back somersault in a pike position. I'm guessing these fellows were swinging, or doing handstands, before what looks like a grand finale.**

Relna Brewer holds Betty Greding on the first workout pad at Muscle Beach in 1937.

"We always just called it Santa Monica Beach," she says. "It wasn't until later, maybe during the war, that other people started calling it Muscle Beach."

Others recall the name coming into the southern California vernacular in the late thirties or early forties. Les Stockton, a lifeguard from 1935 to 1939, always referred to it as Muscle Beach, he says. He recalls UCLA coach Cecil Hollingsworth, an initial instructor at the Beach, doing the same as early as 1936. Irving "Mousey" Cohen, an undefeated college gymnast, said he can remember saying "Let's go to Muscle Beach" as early as 1938. A 1947 issue of *Pageant* magazine corroborated Mousey's memory when it introduced a photo essay on Muscle Beach this way:

> On these and following pages are pictured some of the least inhibited persons in America: habitues of a strip of Santa Monica, California, known as Muscle Beach. This sandy stretch of public property fronting a usually littered boardwalk, got its unofficial designation about nine years ago, when well-muscled youths from nearby Los Angeles began putting on free stunts for passersby.

"We always resented the name," notes Paul Brewer. "The real people attracting the crowds were the gymnastic people." But the name outlasted the resentment—the Beach has become a symbol for much more than the physiques of those of us who worked out and performed there.

BUILDING THE BEACH

What children and adults alike found at Muscle Beach was a circus beneath a blue sky instead of a tent. Even the real circus was limited to three rings. At the Beach, you might see three or more acts performing or practicing on the platform alone. At the same time, you could watch gymnasts honing their skills on the bars or performing somersaults from the rings. You'd see men and women balancing on top of each other, like human pyramids. You'd see the girls flying through the air, then being caught by strong men—movements called "adagio." Other

▽ One of the earliest photos of the Beach is of Relna Brewer holding Betty Greding and the professional act, the Knight Sisters.

men, known as "spotters," the human equivalent of circus nets, stood by to protect the performers.

Between 1935 and 1936, word of mouth was making the Beach a weekly destination for many. Although not as wide in the early days, the Beach was ideally located with the ocean stretching out to its west. A few hundred feet to the north, the Santa Monica Pier shielded the Beach and its inhabitants from harsh wind. To the south was endless sand, to the east, Santa Monica, and beyond that, glorious Hollywood. The entire area probably measured no more than two hundred square yards. Along the Beach, interspersed with soft drink and hamburger stands, areas were delineated for platforms, equipment storage, and a weightlifting pen.

As interest in the activities at their beach continued to grow, Brewer, Pfeiffer and Niederman went to the city officials over and over again to request a larger platform. In 1938 the city of Santa Monica was still saying no, but the local WPA office agreed to provide used lumber. Private donors contributed new lumber, and the work began.

This second platform, about three feet off the ground and about ten by forty feet long, was built extending north to south. This became the spot where real

⬥ Relna Brewer works out on the high rings in 1937.

shows took place. On any given weekend, there were almost as many people in the air, off their feet, as there were standing on the ground.

"That platform was always packed," recalled former Mr. Universe John Grimek, who frequently visited from York, Pennsylvania. "It was a free show."

The equipment attracted more kids needing a free place to work out. College students from UCLA and USC joined them. Before long, an equipment shack was built to hold checkerboards, Ping-Pong, volleyballs and nets. As volleyball became more popular, courts extended toward the ocean, located side by side and to the south of the second workout plat-form. John Kornoff, who would later see his own muscular image on the cover of *Look* magazine, remembers Muscle Beach as "an outdoor gymnasium."

Relna Brewer poses for a news-reel as she prepares to tear in half a telephone book *Movietone News*, here, was just one of the news agencies that frequented Muscle Beach.

Kornoff was first driven to the Beach by one of his older brothers in 1933. Raised in The Flats, a primarily Russian immigrant housing development in east Los Angeles, Kornoff was already involved with his high school gymnastics team. When he saw all of those high school and college kids doing stunts at the Beach, he turned to his brother and sighed, "What a place." In '33, however, only twenty acrobats, at most, were showing up regularly at the Beach and those who did were performing stunts on the rug. Throughout the following year, more and more like John Kornoff began to find their way by word of mouth or by accident.

Although a healthy and well-supported sport in Europe, gymnastics had yet to be taken seriously in America. Most of the "coaches" were teachers haphazardly assigned to the gym team. Glenn Berry, one of the only true gymnastics coaches in Los Angeles, had been in the 1928 Olympics and taught at Polytechnic High. But mentors like him were a rarity—most of the time we taught each other.

At Belvedere Junior High I was lucky to work with Harry Spencer, an excellent tumbling coach. He cared, and gave me some solid advice about technique

⬦ In the early days, spectators made the activities at the Beach even more exciting. As their numbers grew, those who loved watching the free show were part of the reason that it had to end.

⬦ Here I am, in a backbend on the high side of the platform at Muscle Beach.

and balance. My Roosevelt High School football coach was not so advanced. He told my teammates, in front of me, "I don't care if that crazy Zinkin lifts weights. If I ever see any of you doing that, you're off the team." I defied him by placing tops in tumbling and finishing third at an all-city meet in 1939. The reporter who covered the story for our school newspaper wrote that I had "the build of a weightlifter and the agility of a cat."

(My old football coach went on to become principal of Belmont High in the sixties. At that time he called me at my office in Fresno to order a Universal machine for his school. "The least I can do is to order it from you," he said. Our score was settled. Like many coaches of his time, he ultimately learned that building strength didn't mean sacrificing flexibility. Although it didn't carry the same stigma as weightlifting, gymnastics was also a mystery to most of the country at that time.)

While not all of the kids at school shared my enthusiasm about weightlifting and bodybuilding, at the Beach I was fully accepted, as was everyone who walked onto the sand and was willing to learn. We were glad to be sharing information about fitness and hoped that it would be passed on. What was happening at Santa Monica then was becoming a way of life.

THE PERFECT FORM

As the amount of equipment increased, so did the quality of the tricks. At the horizontal bar, it was natural to try a kip-up. That is, hanging by your hands, you'd raise then quickly lower your legs to give you the momentum to come up into a handstand. From a kip-up, you could perform a giant swing, toes pointed, again using your legs for momentum. The trick was also performed on the parallel bars: the athlete would let go of one bar and catch another. That version is now part of Olympic gymnastic routines.

The most common workouts you might see on the Beach were adagio, hand-balancing and gymnastics, which included tumbling, back flips, handstands and ring and parallel bar routines. On the rings, people like Paul Brewer were accomplished at triple flyaways

A bookend pyramid at Muscle Beach. I'm next to the top on the left, and Glen Sundby is the top man on the right. This requires intricate and precise timing and has to be done so that everyone gets to the finish position promptly.

I'm holding super-limber Rosalie Unger, Paula Unger's older sister, in a backbend handstand. What flexibility!

▽ Justice Motter holds Relna
Brewer in a high hand-to-hand.

(three somersaults in the air before landing), while others like Johnny Kornoff stuck to doing doubles (two spins).

One of the most popular acts—for both performers and the crowds—was the adagio. This refers to the ballet-like movements (adagio means "slow movement") of, usually, the male lifting a female partner up over his head, while she strikes a balletic pose such as an "arabesque" or a "bird." Once this was achieved, the man would then pitch his partner into the air, sending her sailing into the arms of a "catcher." When done correctly, it appeared to be performed with such grace and ease, void of any real effort. But of course, that was the illusion of the trick.

"The excitement came in just being able to fulfill a trick," said Relna. "What we were really trying to do was to learn perfect form. Like a diver, you have to learn perfect form. If you don't hold your form, you can't be caught right. Holding your form—that's the secret."

Young girls who came to the Beach wanting to "learn to fly" were taught by the older, more experienced athletes. Initially, they learned three basic adagio movements: the bird (a swan-dive position), the arabesque (leaning forward from the hip with one arm and leg extended in air) and the one-arm lift. In this, the top person has her back to the lifter. The lifter puts his hand on her back, below the waist, takes hold of her ankle and lifts her into the air. It's important that she has a bent knee that straightens and holds firm as she's being lifted. In any of these positions, once lifted above her partner's shoulders, a girl would then have her chance to fly through the air.

Barney Fry, a longtime regular at the Beach and inventor of exercise machinery, masterminded the act of balancing three grown men on the backs of young girls. Of course the girls weren't really lifting the men. He taught the girls to

△ **Paul Brewer, who started what became known as Muscle Beach, performs an iron cross on the rings.**

▷ **Paul Brewer at eighteen. Those who were there say Brewer, his friend Jim Pfeiffer and mechanic Al Niederman were the first to start using the beach for gymnastics.**

lock their legs so that the men could simply rest on their frames, really their hip structures. It made a good picture for tourists because people weren't expecting it.

There were also a lot of hand-to-hand and foot-to-hand balancing acts that moved from the realm of adagio into acrobatics. For example, someone would step into a hand and be thrown into the air to do a somersault or two. Here, strength more than grace was a necessity for both the men and women. Ideas for new and unique positions came about as we experimented to see how high, how fast we were capable of going. Although some of these tricks could be dangerous, we pretty much knew who had more strength and talent and who had less, so that no one was expected to do anything that was beyond his or her skill.

Spotters were also essential in preventing injuries and keeping a good safety record at the Beach. They stood on the sidelines ready to come to the aid of a routine gone astray. We all took turns being spotters for each other. During my whole time at Muscle Beach, save for a few bumps and bruises, I never observed a serious injury.

The other crowd pleasers were the three- and four-high pyramids that we invented to entertain and challenge ourselves. It was a lot of hard work to perfect a combination—there were people falling and catching all the time. "The bottom man, or understander, was the strong man who holds everybody up," said Glenn Sundby who helped in pyramid-building. "Then there's the middle man and it's the top man who does the hand stands up in the air, on top of everybody. In the history of the circus, the bottom man did all the balancing work and the top man was very stiff."

Weightlifting and bodybuilding as a popular spectacle sport didn't really come to the Beach until after World War II. During the thirties, however, several people brought their own weights and both men and women used them to build up their strength as a means to accomplish acrobatic routines.

The tricks we learned, invented and dreamed about would be tried over and over again until we were able to hold a position for maybe a few seconds, maybe a minute. Practices were squeezed out after school and on weekends. Then we might try one out on a Sunday crowd. If we got a few claps we figured it was a good trick. But the applause wasn't our motivation. It just told us that we were making progress.

That's Moe Most under Johnny Kornoff who's supporting Mousey Cohen's handstand and a back lever.

▲ Wayne Long and Russ Saunders in a one-arm handstand. Notice how Russ holds his fingers together. You'll catch only the most skilled professionals in this position. When doing such a stunt, most people will spread their fingers apart or clinch them.

▶ Paula Unger displays the form that made her a top stunt woman. That's Russ Saunders catching her. In their work, such grace came very naturally to them.

CHAPTER TWO

DON'T CALL US MUSCLEHEADS

"This was all new to me. I'd never seen anything like it."
—Pudgy Stockton

Like attracted like. Muscle Beach and its equipment lured athletes to perform and to watch others perform. In those days before the war, acrobatics dominated the Beach. Adagio combined the hard-nosed skills of somersaults and tumbling and added beauty with the graceful elements of dance. You didn't just toss your partner. You sailed her like a kite, and she landed, whether on the ground or in your outstretched arms, like a ballerina.

It wasn't long before contests prevailed. Who (next to the unchallenged Jack LaLanne) could do the most pushups? Who could do the most bar dips or carry a hundred-thirty-five-pound weight overheard the farthest down the Beach. At the time, our competitive natures were just flexing their muscles—although we still didn't care for the term "muscleheads."

By the late thirties, the Beach was drawing weekend crowds in the thousands.

◀ **Eight gymnasts demonstrate precision balance in this 1947 shot.**

Ran Hall, in hat, and Russ Saunders prepare to catch Paula Unger, the "bird" flying at Muscle Beach.

Yet, despite the throngs of people, the core group of performers numbered about fifty or sixty. Some of us were just regular people, others carried sparks that would make them legends. But regardless of what paths we were to take, we all felt like members of an exclusive club or, as many of us still say, "like family."

BEACH REGULARS

At the head of our family in the early days of the Beach was Johnnie Collins. A Russian circus performer, and excellent ice skater, he lived in the same neighborhood as John Kornoff. Collins worked as a lifeguard at Bimini Plunge and was a top stuntman in films with Martha Raye and other stars. Relna Brewer remembers that he taught her to skate, and that when she was thrown across a swimming pool in a film, he caught her.

Collins, whose real last name was Kulikoff, had blue eyes, sandy-blond hair, and pink-white skin that he protected with long baggy pants and a cap. All agreed that he was one of the most generous with his time and talents. It was Collins who guided me through some of my early lessons at Muscle Beach. (In most references to him, you'll see his name spelled as "Johnny," but I have an autographed photo and prefer to spell his name as he did.) Johnnie was older than most of us, and he had more patience and strength than anyone else we knew. To me, he was the first professor of body motion at Muscle Beach.

He was also considered the father of adagio, teaching the young girls the proper techniques for a "birdie" and other positions. During his strenuous workouts, kids would beg him to perform some of his more adventurous tricks, and he would employ them to serve as his partners in adagio and other balancing acts.

Deforrest "Moe" Most was one of the first to discover Muscle Beach and personified the spirit of the Beach in those days. Broad-shouldered and handsome, he had dark shoulder-length hair that gave him a Tarzan-like appearance. Moe made his first visit to the Beach in 1934 while he was still a student at Belmont High School in Los Angeles. Attracted by the equipment, he returned every weekend and began taking part in human pyramids and performing handstands and other acrobatic tricks on rugs in the sand.

Moe was a strong and patient understander. I always felt secure with him at the base of any stunt. He was also great with the youngsters who wanted to learn. He was so good, in fact, that Charles McMillan, who served as director of Muscle Beach from 1944 to 1958, recommended in 1947 that Moe share his

Glenn "Whitey" Sundby leaps over Bruce Conner and Pudgy Stockton, to land in a handstand on partner Wayne Long. Les Stockton said that he was the first performer with whom Whitey ever completed a handstand.

This photo was taken about 1935 just south of Muscle Beach. It was the end of the era of indoor swimming pools that were hot, humid and sort of fun to go into. For many of us, the pools were recreation; we went the way others might go to a bar or a dance. Notice the audience: the men in suits and hats mingling with others in swimsuits. The girl on top is doing an arabesque, something I didn't see until around 1938 or 1939.

⬥ This shot, taken in 1941, shows Don Brown, middle, with fellow pre-med students Coyne Knight, left, and P. J. Moore.

▷ Pudgy Stockton balances Don Brown and goes hand-to-hand with Johnny Kornoff.

position as co-director. Moe remained at the Beach until it closed in late 1958.

John Kornoff was performing tricks in junior high school that most high school students couldn't do. He was my first great inspiration, as he was to many others. He was the youngest person to execute a double flyaway somersault off of the horizontal bar—a trick that landed him in the hospital before he perfected it. Captain of our gymnastics team at Roosevelt High, he was named best gymnast in the city during his sophomore and junior years. In those days, he was already doing double flyaway somersaults off the rings, a trick that entailed literally flying from the rings and completing two somersaults before he landed on his feet. But always looking for a greater challenge, Johnny wanted to take the trick to the horizontal bar, which required great height and perfect timing. Shortly after he turned fourteen, he told his friends in east Los Angeles, "If they ever have new sawdust at Pecan Playground, I'm going to do a double flyaway." A few weeks later, Kornoff got the word. There was sawdust at the neighborhood park.

Kornoff began with a couple of singles with a tuck. "Then I held my tuck a little longer, and there was my double."

It was the first double flyaway off the bars that the Muscle Beach gang had ever seen, and Kornoff did it without a spotter. When he attempted the same trick in the semi-final city meet at Lincoln High, he had a problem in his first routine, however. He caught his foot on the bar, which stopped his spin and forced him into a somersault-and-a-half. He dropped seven or eight feet straight, head first, onto the hardwood floor. But there was no stopping Johnny. He regained consciousness and completed the second routine on the high bar, rings and long horse. He took first place with a perfect double flyaway. Specifically because of Kornoff's accident, however, the trick was declared illegal by the AAU in 1937 and remained so until the fifties.

Say Gold's Gym, and you're really talking about Joe Gold, a bodybuilder, stuntman and member of the original Mae West Show before he opened his original Gold's Gym. Bodybuilders from everywhere, including Arnold Schwarzenegger, trained at Joe's place. But long before his name was emblazoned on T-shirts, Joe was a kid from east Los Angeles and one of my best friends. We were still in junior high when he created a gym in our neighborhood on City Terrace Drive. The Dugout Athletic Club got its name because it was carved into the side of the hill in some property Joe's folks owned.

Born and raised in Los Angeles, he visited Ocean Park Beach when he was six years old. By age twelve, Joe had heard one too many insults from his sister's boyfriend who called him "little fat boy." Thinking that exercise might help, he made his own weights and started the Dugout Gym in an old garage in front of the family home in east Los Angeles.

Though I'd previously visited the Beach with Abe Regenbogen and Johnny Kornoff, my real infatuation began when Gold, Bob Tucker and I went to Muscle Beach together in 1939 and began to seriously work out.

I have an early photograph, taken under the pier, of a human pyramid, where we were trying to teach Gold to be a top man. We couldn't get him to let go of the pier railing. He much preferred volleyball and was a self-diagnosed "beach bum." As much as anyone I know, he loved that Beach. With his broad shoulders, wide smile and tight jeans, he was known to all of us as "Lil Abner."

One performer not afraid to show off his skill was Russ Saunders, arriving in southern California from Canada in 1939. Handsome, with a dancer's grace, he already looked like the swashbuckler roles he would later play as Hollywood's leading stuntman. Among the new friends he met was USC athlete Ran Hall, who worked out at Muscle Beach and introduced him to the crowd there.

Saunders and Relna Brewer created original routines together. Later he worked with Paula Unger in adagio, teeter board—in which one person jumps onto the high end of the board to propel the person standing on the other end into space— and risley. A teeter board may or may not be part of risley, which involves a performer jumping or being pushed into the air and landing on his or her feet or on someone else. Russ also acted as a catcher and a spotter whenever needed.

Glenn Sundby always says he was a weak kid who couldn't succeed in school acrobatics until he learned how to control his body with the rest of us—at Muscle Beach. Soon, however, this kid was part of a professional hand-balancing act, the Wayne-Marlin Trio, that performed all over the country. Muscle Beach gave him purpose and ultimately a successful career. This self-proclaimed onetime runt eventually hand-walked his way into the record books after someone spied him hand walking down the stairs of a hotel where he was appearing. Word got around and Glenn conquered all eight hundred ninety-eight stairs of the Washington Monument—yes, on his hands.

A student at University High in west Los Angeles, Sundby was a member of the gym team but didn't do well because of health problems that included asthma. After school he worked for a wholesale grocer in the Santa Monica area and discovered the Beach while making a delivery to the restaurants there.

"Once I saw the place, I just started coming down," he said. "I'd swing on the

bars. I started meeting people. I was the smallest guy in school for a long time. I can't say enough about the Beach and what it did for me." In addition to his handstands and hand-balancing workouts, he participated in perfect two- and three-high pyramids. In 1939, he finished third on the parallel bars out of forty-five schools.

At Muscle Beach, Sundby met Les Stockton, his girlfriend Pudgy Eville, and Bruce Conner, and was invited to join their group. Stockton was the first to lift him to a handstand, Sundby said. "We'd work out all day long. Pretty soon I was strong enough to pick up people as well as do top work." Friendly and well-liked, Sundby was soon a Muscle Beach regular. Nicknames abounded in those days, and they helped make this group of strangers part of the Muscle Beach club. Sundby didn't stay "Glenn" for long. Stockton surveyed his blond hair that stood out dramatically against his tan and dubbed him "Whitey," a name that has stayed with him for life.

Whitey also met Wayne Long, who became his acrobatic partner in the forties. Sundby, long the keeper of the Muscle Beach archives, had a successful performing career, including a stint as part of first a duo and then a trio of acrobats with the New York-based show of comedic musician Spike Jones. He later covered the Olympics for one of the various magazines he founded. Yet Sundby's memories and loyalties focus on Muscle Beach, and he serves both as if gratefully attempting to repay a major debt.

Arnie Klein was one of the younger members of the group who would ride in my Model A on those weekly workout trips to Santa Monica. By 1945, '46 and '47, he was the first, and, as far as we knew, the only gymnast to win three consecutive city championships in Los Angeles. "Gymnastics was a hobby and it was a love," Klein said. But his abilities weren't limited to that love. He was an all-city high jumper, sprinter and broad jumper at Roosevelt High School, and in 1948, he made a Ripley's book for taking first place in one hundred five consecutive gym meets. When he was inducted into the Jewish Athletic Hall of Fame in 1994, no one could put him in a category. They finally settled on gymnastics, which pleased Klein. "I've done a lot at very high levels," Klein said. "There's nothing tougher than acrobatics. There's nothing tougher than gymnastics."

You didn't have to be big to make a big impression on the Beach. Mousey Cohen, the smallest man on the 1940 gym team at City College, was undefeated, as the local paper reported, "and never missed a meet due to illness or any other liability, which is quite a record." He and Johnny Kornoff never missed a sunny day on the Beach either. They'd park Cohen's Model A Ford in front of Roosevelt High School, in east Los Angeles, and they'd look up at the sun, and look at each other, "and away we'd go." The next day, there would be a note. "Dear Mrs. Jones: Please excuse John and Irv and all the rest of them. They had a terrible cold." "How's your cold?" the teacher would ask Mousey the next day. "That suntan you've got—I hope that cures it."

High school kids weren't the only ones flexing and toning at Muscle Beach. Around 1935, the city of Santa Monica hired UCLA coach Cecil Hollingsworth to teach gymnastics at Muscle Beach. He was one of the early instructors who brought with him professional knowledge of gymnastics that he was more than willing to share with young beach goers. Almost immediately, many of his student athletes, including Bruce Conner, followed.

"He learned the high bar after college and became a super gymnastic coach," Bruce Conner notes. "He was like a father to me. I just loved him."

Conner was one of the gymnasts who'd ride to the Beach every weekend in the back of Hollingsworth's Model A Ford. He moved from Montana to southern California in 1933. With his dark-brown hair and almost aristocratic air, Conner resembled actor Alan Ladd.

At Hollywood High, he joined the gym team, and specialized in rope climbing. Although he weighed only one hundred ten pounds when he graduated from high school, Conner had a lot of strength in his legs and fell in love with hand-to-hand balancing.

He won the Pacific Coast Championship in gymnastics for his phenomenal hand-to-hand balancing. Gymnastics, however, was only the beginning for him. Conner had a cause. Since junior high, he knew that he wanted to establish a rehabilitation center—a revolutionary idea for the times. When he was in seventh and eighth grades, *Strength and Health* magazine was his Bible, Conner said.

His goal, when he entered UCLA, was medical school. That's where he met

Don Brown. Medicine was also Don Brown's goal. He discovered Muscle Beach in 1936, when he began the pre-med program at UCLA. He also met Les Stockton and Ran Hall and, along with Conner, they introduced him to Muscle Beach.

"I never even touched the water," Brown said. "We'd just do tricks all day long."

Soon four of the UCLA gym team members who frequented Muscle Beach decided to form their own hand-balancing group on the side. The Four Aces, composed of Brown, Stockton, Conner and Bob Cockburn, went on to play at the famed Coconut Grove in Los Angeles and at different spots in the San Francisco Bay Area. Brown, certain that he wanted to be a doctor, never considered going professional. The others did.

Les and his future wife, the dramatically misnamed "Pudgy," were one of the best-known Muscle Beach couples. They began dating in 1934, and in 1936 Les, a fun-loving, joke-telling blond, started working out with Pudgy's brother Tony. A UCLA student in 1937, Stockton worked as a life-guard at the Del Mar Club

◁ **Russ Saunders and Paula Unger Boelsems practiced routines that they later took around the world.**

▷ **The monkey man Johnny Robinson was Olympic material for his balancing and horizontal bar acumen.**

Russ Saunders later posed for Salvador Dali and became a leading stuntman.

↟ **Pat McCormick before winning several gold medals in Olympic diving, balances Whitey Sundby.**

just three hundred or so yards from Muscle Beach. During 1937 and 1938, Les, Pudgy and Bruce Conner formed a hand-balancing act, the Rennoc Trio (Conner spelled backward). They were good, they were in demand, and they were booked almost every week.

The athletes learned much more than gymnastics at the Beach. Many of them filled in when the traveling or circus professionals were short a partner. They literally rubbed elbows with a diverse and talented group.

"Bob Waterfield was on our gym team at UCLA and was a fabulous quarterback," Stockton said. "Jane Russell was around all the time, but we didn't think about her as more than a very pretty girl who happened to be Waterfield's girlfriend." Waterfield, who played football for San Fernando High against Kornoff at Roosevelt High, went on to play for the Los Angeles Rams and to work as their coach. Bob Leonard, a research physicist, at UCLA, and Gordon McRae, later the Redondo Pier developer, both worked as bottom men for many of the Muscle Beach stunts.

"We had coaches and ex-gymnasts from the '32 and '36 Olympic games," said Conner. "Everyone at the Beach wasn't a bunch of dopes. You could be a butcher or a Ph.D. It was a great mixing ground."

SUITABLE WOMEN

Not only was the public naive about weightlifters—it was extremely naive about women who chose to lift weights, work out, or do anything other than pursue marriage or careers. That didn't stop the women of Muscle Beach. On the Beach, skill, not gender, helped to level the playing field, and for many of those early women, it provided the chance to prove themselves. Some males liked and admired what they saw. Others chose to ridicule it. They heckled. They jeered. And of course they challenged the sexual orientation of the women, especially when the women didn't show much interest in them.

At five feet one-half inch, Relna Brewer was the first woman weightlifter from

Muscle Beach to receive publicity. Small and blond, she had delicate, attractive features, and a well-proportioned, strong body. At the time, in fact, she was dubbed the strongest woman in the world, but that was just public relations talk, she said.

When she was seventeen, she worked in California's first health food store, which was located in Santa Monica. It was her job, using a large fruit press, to squeeze the carrot, celery, watermelon, spinach and oranges into juice. Because the woman who owned the shop couldn't pay much, she offered to trade. So Brewer drank a lot of carrot juice.

Brewer first came to the Beach with her brother Paul, who thought that working out would help to improve the poor health she suffered. When she was eleven, she was severely burned by boiling water in a home accident. Her back looked like a relief map, and her right shoulder was four inches lower than her left. At first, she'd just hang on the bars at Muscle Beach and stretch her scar tissue until it hurt, she recalls.

The Beach helped her regain her health. With Al Niederman's training and lots of work on her own, she could finally stand up straight. She liked doing giant swings by putting her leg over the bar on top and going over and over and over—at least fifty-eight

◈ **Les and Pudgy Stockton were married in 1941. In addition to the hundreds of articles that featured photographs of her, Pudgy Stockton appeared on more than forty magazine covers around the world.**

swings the time she counted, she said. She performed her first flyaway somersault on the small rings at age sixteen. After they built the high rings, she did it on those, and found it far easier. Although the claims of who was first to do what may vary, Relna remembers watching Chester Hill do the first triple flyaway off of the high rings. Paul, her brother, did the second triple flyaway, she said.

Once when Relna and her friend Pudgy Stockton were lifting weights on the Beach, they were stopped by shouts from a heckler whom Relna remembers as a wimpy little guy.

"Fake, fake," he yelled. "You can't tell me that weighs anything."

"Why don't you come on up and show us how to do it," Relna suggested, placing her one-hundred-thirty-five-pound barbell on the platform.

The man followed through with the dare, convinced that he was right, and of course, he couldn't even lift the weight. Relna, along with Barney Fry, a physical culturist who operated the Elks Club gym, spent two years at the Beach training future Olympic diving champion Pat McCormick, who became the only woman diver in Olympic history to win four gold medals back to back.

In 1939, Relna landed a job as a swimmer at the World's Fair in San Francisco, after which she planned to travel with the Ice Follies. Her plans took a detour when she met and married Gordon McRae, a builder/developer, whom she introduced to the Beach. He became a reliable understander. Later she worked for many years in a Santa Monica medical clinic.

Pudgy Stockton, nicknamed by her family at age five when she was still Abbye Eville, began dating Les Stockton in the fall of 1934. He ultimately brought her to Muscle Beach, where she was introduced to adagio and human pyramids.

"This was all new to me," she said. "I'd never seen anything like it."

She graduated from high school in 1935 and went to work for the telephone company, where she stayed more than seven years. The sedentary job contributed to a weight gain, and she began training with weights. She worked split shifts, four hours on, and four hours off, and during her off-time went down to the Beach to practice handstands. As she continued lifting weights, her body found its perfect form.

◁ **From the bottom, Wayne Long, Bruce Conner and Pudgy Stockton, with Glenn Sundby on top.**

◇ **Jimmy Starkey performs a one-arm handstand on his wife Kay, supported by me.**

The blond weightlifter was a petite five feet one-and-a-half inches, but she soon had the most dramatic female body on the Beach. Winner of many awards then and now (most recently the third Steve Reeves International Society Pioneer Award in July of 1998), Pudgy says she most treasures the comment by 1944 Mr. America Steve Stanko that she was "a female John Grimek."

Pudgy married Les Stockton in 1941. As early as 1939, she started receiving mail from various readers of magazines and newspapers all over the world. *Pic*, a photo magazine similar to *Look*, spotted her while covering an article on the UCLA gym team. In 1939, she appeared on the magazine's cover being tossed through the air by Bruce Conner, while Les waited to catch her.

Paula Unger and her older sister, Rosalie, first discovered Muscle Beach in 1934, shortly after moving from Denver. For two weeks, their family lived in an apartment in Santa Monica.

"One day, my sister and I wandered along the Beach, and I saw these people flying off the bars." Paula recognized the trick as one she had learned in tumbling class in Colorado and approached the man performing it, asking, "Hey, Mister. Would you do that with me?"

He did, she did, and that, Paula said, was that. She was hooked.

But it was a year before she returned to the Beach again, this time with her protective mother, Clayton Unger, who not only drove her there but became a member of the coordinating council for the city of Santa Monica. Mrs. Unger joined with regulars such as Moe Most and argued successfully that the city funnel some of the recreation department money being used for oceanside concerts. At that time, there was no cement, and football games took place in the sand.

Paula rapidly progressed from a little eight-year-old begging people to teach her tricks, to a bright, graceful young woman sailing through the air—"our bird," as many of the others still call her.

"She was so sleek," Arnie Klein recalls. "They threw her around like a toy."

With little or no money to spend, Paula would often stop by Little Audrey's Malt Shop, where she could visit with Audrey and her husband Westley, while enjoying the drink of the day, a pine float—a toothpick in a glass of water.

Others on the Beach treated her like a little sister. They spotted for her, and except for one time in her teens, she cannot recall falling. Paula was one of the youngest of the Muscle Beach crowd that included three girls who like her were eight to nine years old, and one five-year-old. Yet she never worried for her safety, she said. "Times were different then. No one ever put a hand on me." At less than five feet and eighty pounds, she was fearless, fun-loving and eager to learn.

As an adult, she worked with Russ Saunders, became a stunt woman, earned her bachelor's and master's degrees, and along with Glenn Sundby, became a founding member of the Sports Acrobatic Association in the United States. To this day, I can always recognize Paula, regardless of how the camera catches her. I look only at the hands and feet. Hers are easy to distinguish because they're as graceful and well posed as if she is dancing on solid ground instead of in the air. While others were the embodiments of strength, Paula and Russ were like dancers—grace and strength combined.

Kay Crosson was fourteen or fifteen when she first went to the Beach. There was just a mat, no platform, she said. "Old Lady Giroux ran the playground, and she was so strict. You couldn't sit down. You worked out or got off of the play-ground."

She used to sneak to Muscle Beach because she knew her strict mother would never permit it. For Kay, who had always been shy, the Muscle Beach crowd provided the confidence she needed. "They were family, no, more than family, because there wasn't any criticism there," she said. "They were all pulling for you."

Kay met Jim Starkey, another Beach body-builder, on the Santa Monica Pier when she was sixteen. While her parents, conveniently out of eyesight, relaxed on a bench, she noticed Jim who was preparing to go for a dive. He smiled at Kay. She smiled back. Then she captivated him by demonstrating that she wasn't like any woman he'd ever met. "I stood on my head and spun,

Pudgy Stockton's body was so perfect that people on the Beach called her "the female John Grimek."

then raced him on my hands down the Beach," she said. "I almost won."

Married in 1938, the Starkeys spent every spare moment on the Beach. "We were always down there. That was our weekend," she said. The Starkeys developed a muscle act, which required great strength on Kay's part, and they performed all over the southern California area and throughout the state. Often Kay would lift Jim to her shoulders at the end of the act, but the audience just saw them as a cute couple and applauded, even if she did something as simple as pose.

Dodie Abro, a professional dancer before she moved to California and mar-

⬦ **The women who competed to be Miss Muscle Beach in the mid-1940s were all so beautiful that sometimes it was difficult to concentrate.**

ried Muscle Beach regular Holger Wahlgren Abro (known as Wally the Swede), later performed as an acrobat with him for everyone from the Queen of England to King Farouk. Encouraged by her mother, she began dancing at age three and had performed as a professional dancer at USOs before she visited Muscle Beach with her gymnastics trainer, Sam Mintz. After she and Abro fell in love, they agreed that they wanted to work together. Combining their skills in ballet and acrobatics, the pair traveled the world together. Until discovering Muscle Beach, she had felt like an anomaly, Abro remembered.

"Up to that point, women just didn't do those things," she said. "I think that Muscle Beach changed a lot of people's ideas of what a woman could do if given the opportunity."

Other women on the Beach included: Rosie Unger (Paula's older sister), an excellent tumbler; Stella Sams, a weightlifter; Edna Rivers, a weightlifter who also did stunt work; Evelyn Smith, a strong blonde who taught swimming, did stunt work, and broke water-skiing records by skiing to Catalina Island and back; and Bunny Waters, a Santa Monica lifeguard, whose beauty and strength made her a role model for many young women.

"We all worked together. We helped each other," Relna recalls. "The men treated us right. We all had a good time seeing how much we could accomplish."

BEACH LEGENDS

Local talent, impressive as it was, played an important yet relatively small part of what was to become the international success story of Muscle

⬦ **In this three-high, Lynwood Ganzon is doing a handstand, with Bill Robson (Dolly's husband) on the bottom.**

Beach. Athletes from all over the world were drawn there. Performers exchanged stories as they traveled across the country and the world. Our Beach made a great setting for freelance photographers who shot for the strength magazines. Writer Earle Liederman and photographer Cecil Charles collaborated on articles about the Beach that ran in top physical culture magazines. Many readers around the world first glimpsed the Beach through their work. In addition, members of various internationally known vaudeville acts visited the Los Angeles Athletic Club gym to work out between shows. Their first Beach hangout was located north of the Ocean Park Pier.

The reputation of Muscle Beach grew, and along with that, the legends. Muscle Beach didn't attract just kids looking for a way to kill time. Many of those watching the show were better known than the performers. Two-time Mr. America winner John Grimek was a hero on the Beach. (After he won the title twice in a row, the American Athletic Union changed its rules so that a candidate could win only once.) Grimek said other athletes asked him about the Beach even when he was as far away as Europe for the 1936 Olympics (in weightlifting). That he would choose to represent our Beach validated what was happening there, making the Muscle Beach regulars proud.

Born in 1909, Grimek ranks with Steve Reeves and Arnold Schwarzenegger when it comes to changing the ideal form for bodybuilders. Dark and broad-shouldered, he proved to the distrusting medical profession that having muscles didn't make one musclebound. Although he visited Muscle Beach only once or twice a year from York, and only as an observer, he was the ideal of the athletes there and everywhere in the thirties, forties, fifties and sixties. Earlier body-builders had a top-heavy look with broad shoulders, big arms and less emphasis on good leg development. Grimek, like Bert Goodrich, the first Mr. America of 1938, had a well-proportioned, symmetrical body with leg size to match. His artistic posing skills enhanced that body, making him look statue-perfect.

Grimek became the U.S. heavyweight lifting champion in 1936 and qualified for the Olympic team, so he traveled to Berlin for the Games. Most of those in the heavyweight class were one hundred or more pounds heavier than he. He finished ninth out of thirteen competitors.

Upon his return to the states, "I headed for the Beach. That was where every-body met," Grimek said. "It's where we discussed everything."

Grimek had plenty to discuss. His southern California friends wanted to hear about his experiences at the Olympics. "Yeah, they wanted to know how I made

⏶ Dodie and Wally (as we called him at the Beach) Abro combined acrobatic skill with their dance movements.

◁ Kay Starkey made it look easy, but the stunts she did in the act with her husband Jimmy required tremendous skill and strength.

out in the games," he said. "They all asked, 'Did you see Hitler?' Yeah, the lousy punk was sitting just above me, but he stormed out of the place when Jesse Owens won."

Grimek's approach was affable and easy-going to the end. Although he must have been aware of his status, he was content to be an enthusiastic onlooker in those early days of Muscle Beach.

The legendary Jack LaLanne helped his reputation along by performing stunts that no one in his right mind would attempt. In the early days of Muscle Beach, his fame spread because of how fast he could burn through one thousand pushups. Considered an odd character in those days, he broke numerous records, offered ten thousand dollars to anyone who could follow him through his work-out routine, and gained plenty of attention—and ridicule.

"I would be six foot seven right now if they hadn't beat me down so much," the five-foot-eight LaLanne said. One of the few places LaLanne felt welcome was Muscle Beach, Santa Monica.

"It was like family," he said. "Everybody was there for a reason, all of those role models. We had the greatest athletes in the world, and everybody would learn from everybody else."

LaLanne worked fourteen hours a day at his gym in Berkeley. He'd close the gym, then drive four hundred miles to get to Muscle Beach. Even after driving all night, he still could and did do it all—weightlifting, hand-balancing, posing contests, pyramids.

Being one of the few vegetarians on the Beach didn't bother LaLanne. He brought his own food, usually apple or carrot juice and vegetables.

Once, the sun went down, LaLanne couldn't just go home and to bed. He again drove all night to get back in time to open his own gym the next morning.

A tale has long made the rounds about how gym entrepreneur Vic Tanny first came to Muscle Beach. As the rumor goes, Tanny, a high school English teacher in New York, went out to dig his car out of the snow one day, grew frustrated, and decided to drive to California without as much as a goodbye to his girlfriend.

"It's a cute story, but he came out in the summer," said his brother, Armand, correcting the long recycled legend.

Although Vic had previously visited, it was Armand who made that first move from New York, knowing that his brother would join him later.

The Tannys shared handsome good looks, Vic, the born promoter, had striking blue eyes, and Armand dark, almost black eyes. Vic began training his brother with weights when Armand was twelve. Although a young competitive weightlifter in New York, Armand never expected to lift another weight when he moved to California to attend UCLA in September of 1939, as a pre-med major.

Armand said he arrived "in the middle of a ferocious heat wave." One evening around nine he went to the Beach to cool off. Then, as he drew nearer, he heard a clatter ringing through the night. Man, he thought, that's a familiar sound.

The sound, of course, was the clanking of weight plates. Even in that heat, that late at night, "I saw people in their bathing suits and their blankets, people doing flyaways on the rings," he said. "I came back the next day."

During 1940 and '41, Armand won the Pacific Coast light heavyweight and heavyweight championships. "I was pointed toward the Olympics at Helsinki," he said, "until Hitler."

Vic Tanny followed his brother to California in 1940, and he and Armand opened Vic Tanny's in Santa Monica that same year. It was the first of eighty-four Vic Tanny gyms across the country. More extravagant than any modern gym, they contained bowling alleys, skating rinks and movie theaters.

Vic was the guilty party who entered me in the first-ever Mr. California contest in 1941, which was held in his gym. A nineteen-year-old kid, I didn't like bodybuilding for posing purposes and told Vic so. I also reminded him that at five feet seven inches, I didn't stand a chance of winning against the giants who were competing with me.

"Your proportions are better than anybody else's," Vic assured me.

I was a kid, and he was a successful gym operator. I did what he said. And I won, over several future Mr. America contenders, including Gene Jantzen, who placed sixteenth, and Eric Pederson, who placed second in the 1942 Mr. America competition. I wouldn't have imagined it possible without that not-so-subtle push from Vic.

As word continued to spread about Muscle Beach, the welcome mat stayed out—for everyone. There was strength, safety and conviction in this group of eager athletes who came together between the Great Depression and World War II. Muscle Beach was our education, our club, our cause. It was our youth.

LOOK

NOVEMBER 17, 1942 10¢ 12¢ IN CANADA
YEARLY SUBSCRIPTION $2.50

Must We Draft Women?

Hitler's Coming Winter in Russia
By MAJOR GEORGE FIELDING ELIOT

PHYSICAL TRAINING
INSTRUCTOR
U. S. ARMY AIR CORPS

⊪–⫪

CHAPTER THREE

WAR COMES TO MUSCLE BEACH

*"The Navy has a good man in Jack LaLanne; his magnificent physique
should inspire some Navy man to aspire to a better build."*
—Tony Terlazzo, *Strength and Health Magazine*, May 1943

In 1939, Germany invaded Poland, and Britain, France, Australia, New Zealand
and Canada declared war on Germany. Hitler swept across Europe, occupying
Denmark, Norway, Paris, the Channel Islands. Italy fell to the fascists. On
December 7, 1941, I woke up to the radio and the news that Japan had
attacked Pearl Harbor and declared war on the United States. I was nineteen years
old. I knew about what had been happening, but I couldn't have imagined the
effect Pearl Harbor would have on me.

◁ John Kornoff, on the cover of *Look* magazine, depicted to the nation, the image of the American serviceman
protecting the country. Fitness became a national phenomenon that continues into the new century.

▷ Hollywood stuntman Russ Saunders doing a one-arm handstand on Johnnie Collins, an acrobat from
Russia. Circus performers often visited Muscle Beach, where they found an eager group of young people to
teach. Johnnie was one of the most popular.

◀ Earl Eads, on disability from the service, was paralyzed from the waist down. After working with me in our Physical Services gym (where this photograph of us was taken), he could lie on a mat and hold me in a handstand. In the background is one of my early inventions.

Stunned and angry, I went looking for my two best friends. When I couldn't locate Joe Gold, I sought out Bob Tucker. His mother, also alarmed by the news, told me that Bob had gone to a matinee, but she couldn't remember which film or which theater.

I soon found him, and we went to the car, where we could talk and plan without distractions. "How can this be happening?" I asked him. "So many of our friends are Japanese."

"This is different," he said. His words felt right. I was trying to make sense out of something that defied reason, as only war can. The term *kamikaze* echoed in my mind.

"Let's try to go together," I said, "you and Joe and me." I punctuated the statement with some ritualistic swearing, and he responded in kind.

The last thing I needed was a war. Yet, as I sat in that car on that December day with my friend, I knew I'd gladly go anywhere, do

Stuntman Johnnie Collins holds Dodie Abro in a split balance.

anything, to help my country win. I wasn't alone. Patriotism was as healthy as everything else at Muscle Beach. When the country went to war, most of the Muscle Beach population went with it.

My plans were waylaid by my marriage and the birth of my son, DeWayne. I was finally able to enter the Navy in April 1943, when DeWayne was three months old. Before that, in 1942, the city of Santa Monica called on Muscle Beach people to supply some backup for a war bond promotion program. Russ Saunders, Ran Hall and I volunteered. The city provided us with a flatbed truck trailer, approximately eight by thirty feet. This was our stage. We ad-libbed through fifteen or twenty minutes of hand-balancing positions, on the trailer. I don't know how much money our routine raised for the war, but it raised our spirits.

Although Joe Gold and I originally planned to enlist together, he joined the Coast Guard in 1942; I went into the Navy and signed up for armed guard, wanting to fight. Instead, I was sent to physical instruction and rehabilitation schools, ending up at Long Beach Naval Hospital. My purpose, as it turned out, was not to injure the enemy but to help heal our injured servicemen. I took to the job as if I'd been born for it.

While training for the job at the physical instructor school in Maryland, I was reintroduced to instructor Bruce Conner whom I had first met at Muscle Beach around 1937. We both attended the U.S. Navy's first-ever Rehabilitation School in New York. After the war, Bruce and I used our wartime experiences to open our Physical Services gym in the summer of 1948, making the equipment and weights ourselves.

"Almost everybody rose to the highest," recalls Conner. "The war record of Muscle Beach is second to none. These guys were super warriors. They served the country in the best way possible, and everyone was a leader."

But the men from Muscle Beach would bring something new to both the military and to the fighting fields.

Although an excellent gymnast, John Kornoff attended Washington State College on a football scholarship until war was declared. In 1941, after two years of college, he joined the Army Air Force and became the first physical training instructor at Mitchell Field in New York.

▲ Here are Vic Tanny and John Grimek enjoying some refreshment at Silent Leo's. In the 1940s, John had already been to the Olympics, and Vic was making history with his gyms.

◀ This photograph of a three-stack with a handstand was taken in the late 1940s. I'm the guy next to the top. In this position, I could move the top mounter to help enforce alignment to keep us all from falling backward.

The balancing Knox Trio of Muscle Beach was made up of some of the youngest regulars, circa 1947 and 1948. That's Larry on top, then Billy, then Marylin on the bottom. Their father asked me to train them, and they later turned professional.

I look at this photo, which appears at first glance like great fun, and see the hard work of the skilled participants. Wayne Long is on the bottom, doing a foot-to-foot with Bruce Conner, while Glenn Sundby is holding a shoulder stand on their feet and Pudgy Stockton is doing a handstand. Note Bruce's palm on her heels; he's slowing what had to be a powerful movement to propel Pudgy up there in the first place.

"How would you like to be in Special Services?" his commanding officer asked after he saw him working out on some bars.

"What's Special Services?" Kornoff replied. After listening to the detailed explanation, and realizing that enlisted men would now be training troops as civilians had previously done, he agreed, "That's right up my alley." He became the first military physical trainer used by the Army.

He was able to return on a couple of rare furloughs to Muscle Beach. Kornoff felt lonely there, however. Most of his friends, like him, were in the service, so he didn't recognize most of the new faces at the Beach.

In 1942, Kornoff, who was going through a group of exercises with a rifle in front of three hundred men, was called aside by a photographer who said he worked for *Look* magazine.

"Give me a call," he told Kornoff, and Kornoff did. The photographer invited him to New York City to pose for some photographs and paid him fifty-five dollars.

"It wasn't a great sum of money," Kornoff said, "but in 1942, my pay in the Army was twenty-five dollars a month. I didn't even believe the guy until it came out, and there was my picture splattered all over the place."

Literally splattered, as it turned out. Kornoff's buddies saw the cover before he did. One of his friends called him and said, "Go to the canteen." Once there, he found that cover plastered on every wall and rack within view.

What did that photographer, not to mention the *Look* staff and the rest of the nation see in that photograph? The war was new and Americans needed reassurance in their fighting men. Shirtless, muscles rippling and obviously fit to fight, Kornoff depicted, the American ideal: the perfect man to protect our country.

John Kornoff at Muscle Beach.

Holger Abro holds Russ Saunders in a hand-to-head balance.

Professional Frankie Vincent, "the Mighty Mite" does a handstand.

◇ **Contestants for the Miss Muscle Beach contest.**

Kornoff was one of the few football players who worked out with weights. At one hundred eighty pounds, he was a gymnast with the muscular arms and shoulders of a weightlifter. You can bet he looked better than ninety-nine percent of the guys picking up *Look* magazine that week, yet not so much different that his form seemed unattainable.

I believe that his photo on *Look*'s cover was the beginning of a change of attitude regarding fitness, an attitude that culminated years later in President John F. Kennedy's focus on fitness, which even then seemed revolutionary. As early as May 1943, Dick Bachtell published "Weight Training in the Service," in *Strength and Health*. He said simply, "A great many men use weights to improve themselves physically prior to induction in the service. It makes things easier for them."

It was certainly revolutionary to us to see a Muscle Beach regular glorified instead of vilified. Mousey Cohen, Kornoff's high school buddy and post-war

acrobatic partner, framed the magazine on the spot. He still has it. Bruce Conner
was serving in the Navy when the magazine came out.

"I see a *Look* magazine, and there's my buddy Johnny with a rifle in front of
him and stripped to the waist," he said. "It was a shock."

Other friends were equally surprised and proud that one of our own—and in
a way, we ourselves—were gaining acceptance in a world that had not long before
scoffed at or, at least, ignored what we had exemplified at Muscle Beach.

Gene Smith, a Muscle Beach friend who was a paratrooper, tried to convince
Kornoff to join that branch as an instructor. Kornoff tried but was refused because
of his heavy football-player weight. Smith was later reported missing in action,
one of the few Muscle Beach casualties.

Joe Gold, still known as "Little Abner," was in the Coast Guard from 1942 to
1946. He spent one-and-one-half years in the South Pacific in the middle of the
war, where he saw a lot of action. During one of the bombings, he took a fall that
caused the spinal injuries that, since 1980, have made it necessary for him to use
a wheelchair. ("That doesn't stop me," Gold says. "I don't let anything stop me.")

▲ **Johnny Robinson and Moe
Most on the high bar.**

After the South Pacific, he served in the Aleutian Islands, and for a few months, he was stationed on a military watch on the Santa Monica Pier.

After the war, "I swore I'd collect my 52-20," he said. At that time, veterans could receive twenty dollars per week for fifty-two weeks. It sounded good to Gold, until he remembered that he had to eat. He decided to try the Merchant Marines in which he served from 1948 to 1978.

Armand Tanny joined the Navy but didn't serve long because of an injured leg. As a result of the metal shortage, he was unable to continue in the gym business. Instead he went into the movie business—stunt work as well as bit parts. After finishing his pre-med studies, he attended physical therapy school with Bruce Conner. Later, as a professional wrestler, he traveled all over the United States and visited Hawaii. Tanny loved that world of wrestling.

"It was a wild life, and I was a young bronco," he acknowledges.

War swept everyone into its wake. In 1944, when he was eighteen years old, Steve Reeves received his papers. Before reporting to his unit, he agreed to accompany an Army friend to visit the friend's aunt in the Hollywood area for a week.

At that time, a tram traveled from Hollywood down Sunset Boulevard to the ocean. The young men took it and soon found their way to Muscle Beach. At the Beach, Reeves discovered others like himself who valued and cared for their bodies.

"There were all of these individuals who were like minded in the pursuit of health and physical improvement," he said. "Muscle Beach drew people from all over the U.S. like a magnet, and by example and word of mouth, everyone could benefit from the experience and example of the physique stars. Muscle Beach was the perfect setting for extraordinary people and those who admired them."

Originally from Glasgow, Montana, Reeves had moved to Oakland, California, when he was ten and had worked out with weights since the age of sixteen at Ed Yarick's gym. Yarick later produced two Mr. Americas, Jack Dellinger in 1949 and Reeves in 1947. Yarick and Jack LaLanne were partners in a hand-balancing act on Sunny Cove Beach, Oakland's version of Muscle Beach.

His approach earned Reeves the title of Mr. Pacific Coast in 1946, and in 1947, Mr. Western America and Mr. America. He would go on to be named Mr. World in Cannes, France, in 1948, and Mr. Universe in London in 1950. They were expensive titles, as Reeves had to work to pay for transportation, accommodations and other expenses.

◁ **In this shot, I'm balancing Paula Unger Boelsems.**

Russ Saunders prepares to catch stuntwoman Paula Unger Boelsems.

In those days bodybuilders tended to be in the five-foot-seven-inch to five-foot-eleven-inch range, he said, and they were big, tending toward bulky. At six feet one with classic proportions, Reeves changed all that.

Throughout his week-long stay in Los Angeles and on the Beach, Reeves heard one question over and over: "Are you a movie star?"

If all those people believed he was a movie star, perhaps he should be, he thought. He forgot about Hollywood and went to war.

While he was in the Army, he briefly mulled over the

⬧ That's my son, DeWayne Zinkin, to the right. I know exactly what he's thinking as he watches his big buddy Les Stockton balancing those other kids. He's wondering why he's not in there. He and Les frequently did tricks together. Those of us who had children included them in our activities on the Beach.

◇ Pals Lynwood Ganzon on the left, and DeWayne, my son, on the right, motivated me to come up with a way of balancing two youngsters at one time. The handstand position is more difficult, so it has to take place first. Only then, does DeWayne step from my shoulders into my hand.

idea of trying for a career in the movies, but at the moment, he had more pressing concerns. Thoughts of anything but survival were far away.

The war years changed Muscle Beach in terms of participants. New, younger faces were beginning to show up but enough of the regulars were able to make periodic visits during furloughs or breaks in their jobs. We had succeeded in our goal of teaching and passing on to others what we knew so that workouts continued on the Beach. The general public was hungry for entertainment that distracted them from the war, and weekend crowds still flocked to see the free shows.

During the war, the military used hotels in southern California as housing

centers. As a result, many servicemen from all branches of the service would spend a couple of weeks at the Beach. Practicing the training they learned in their military units, hundreds of soldiers, sailors and Marines did calisthenics from the pier to the Beach. Most of them vowed to return once the war was over, and a surprising number kept those promises.

The Navy was especially prominent at the Beach during the war. Ships would anchor off the Santa Monica Pier and boats would run sailors back and forth. There were also a couple Naval R&R centers in the area, placing the men in proximity to Muscle Beach. Some watched the routines, while others got involved in learning a few of the tricks. And always, they took their stories about Muscle Beach home with them.

⬥ **We called him "Old Man Mering," but he looks pretty fine here, socks and all. Taken in 1939, this shot shows a free-arm plange. This is an impressive stunt for anyone, but especially a sixty-five-year-old.**

Many of the original crowd went to war, or in Don Brown's case, medical school in southern California. Even though he was in school, he kept his Muscle Beach connection throughout medical school by setting up and occasionally performing in shows with friends like Russ Saunders, Moe Most and Jack LaLanne.

Those who didn't fight with the troops entertained them. Glenn Sundby wanted to join the Air Force but was refused because of his asthma. He hooked up with his old partner George Wayne Long, who had been refused because of a bad heart. During the war, Sundby and Long began working with USO road shows and the Stagedoor Canteen in New York. What they had learned at Muscle Beach now became the basis of a career. Theirs was slow-motion balancing, composed of posing, handstands and arches as opposed to flying, spins and catching.

When not entertaining troops, they played Radio City Music Hall and the Roxie and in 1942, Mike Todd's show on Broadway at the Music Box Theatre. As the Wayne-Marlin Trio, they and whatever young woman they could find for the final third of the trio played at the Desert Inn when Las Vegas was little more than a desert. But the women in the trio kept running off to get married. In 1944, Sundby sent for the one person he could trust.

Dolores Sundby, Glenn's sister, was one of the ubiquitous attractive blondes who enjoyed the Beach. As the third member of the Wayne-Marlin Trio, she was literally in her brother's hands, and she credits him for making her look good. As their careers grew, she often repeated to herself one of her brother's favorite lines. "I did it because I didn't know I couldn't." This philosophy carried the Wayne-Marlin Trio through a seventeen-year career.

In 1937, Moe Most took a job at Douglas Aircraft for fifty cents an hour, but continued to return on weekends to Muscle Beach and lived in a government-run hotel. "The Beach got even bigger during the war, because all the soldiers were there, and they worked out," he recalls.

During the war, Moe continued to work in the aircraft industry, most of the time at North American Aircraft, building bombers. Every weekend he could, he walked across the street from his apartment to Muscle Beach. As an acrobat, Moe toured Army and Navy bases, even some prisons. In his spare time, he also created a few firsts of his own.

Moe, Johnny Robinson and Vern Connors were the first to do a triple giant swing on a high bar. Moe said it looked like a three-bladed airplane propeller. Robinson, a fair blond with a wiry gymnast's body, excelled in high-bar routines, including a monkey act, complete with primate-like scratching and movements, on the monkey bars.

In 1941, Moe did forty barehanded giant swings, a stunt previously performed only with hand guards. In 1942, he broke his own record, doing fifty swings, barehanded, of course.

Competitive lifter and bodybuilder Leo Stern was drawn to Muscle Beach around 1941, attracted to the hand-balancing acts. A resident of San Diego, he traveled to Muscle Beach after competing in the Los Angeles area. Occasionally, he'd have an opportunity to work out with the Muscle Beach regulars.

Stern served in the Air Force from 1942 to 1945 and operated a service gym in Las Vegas, Nevada, from 1943 to '44, during which time he developed a weightlifting team. With the exception of parallel bars, his gym lacked the equipment available at Muscle Beach, and he returned when he could, Stern said.

His inspiration was John Grimek, whom he met in the early forties. Encouraged by Grimek, as most were at that time, Stern won Mr. San Diego in 1941 and went on to compete, as I did, in the first Mr. California contest held in Vic Tanny's Santa Monica gym.

◇ **This is an earlier version of the four-high shown on page eight. In this one Gene Miller is on top, but he is held by Russ Saunders and I am on the shoulders of Moe Most, my favorite understander. This stunt required much patience until Miller, Jack LaLanne, Moe and I (as understander) finally perfected it.**

Most of us who participated had never seen a contest. We took our posing ideas from what we saw in the muscle magazines. At nineteen, I was probably the youngest entrant for Mr. California. The majority were in their mid- to late-twenties, and I knew that there was no way I could win. If I could place in the top ten, however, that would be more than enough.

I didn't eat dinner the night before and visualized what poses I should use. I decided to do something from the front and something from the back, and, most important, to execute each transition smoothly. Although I didn't know it then, we were judged by the clarity of our skin, our general appearance, our skill in posing, and how symmetrical our bodies appeared.

I went out, and I posed, smiling into the darkness...then I heard something that stunned me—applause, lots of applause. Maybe I really could place, I thought, as I left the stage. Maybe even get in the top ten—maybe even third. Yes, third. I'd be so grateful for that.

As the judges tallied the points, I went backstage, and Jack LaLanne entertained the crowd by singing "I Believe," and other songs.

Standing in the back of the gym, I suddenly realized how hungry I was. I started to eat a Baby Ruth candy bar, and as I did, I heard Jack stop in mid-song. There was a lull. Still clinging to my hope of finishing in the top ten, I hurried to the men's room and washed my mouth of any telltale chocolate evidence. As I returned, the third-place winner was being announced. Me, me, me, I prayed. Please. The name that pounded in my ears was not mine.

OK, I thought. I got a lot of applause. Maybe, possibly. . .

My heart dropped a foot when they announced the second-place winner, but before I could recover, I recognized the beautiful sound of my own name—Mr. California, Harold Zinkin. I walked, then ran to that stage and accepted my trophy from Pudgy Stockton. Even so, I did my best to look cool and hide the emotions that echoed through me, and I guess I did a pretty good job, for a nineteen-year-old kid.

Perhaps because of the war and its emphasis on strength, the gym business continued to flourish. Following the lead of LaLanne, Tanny and others, Walter Marcyan opened a small gym in the forties on Sunset Boulevard. That's where the personal trainer concept was first developed,

▲ Bruce Conner posing.

◈ Relna Brewer McRae lifting.

◀ Glenn Sundby, just seventeen, is held in a handstand by Pudgy Stockton.

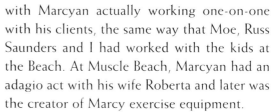

▸ Although I can't yet believe it, Pudgy Stockton hands me the trophy.

▾ Stunned, I become the first Mr. California.

with Marcyan actually working one-on-one with his clients, the same way that Moe, Russ Saunders and I had worked with the kids at the Beach. At Muscle Beach, Marcyan had an adagio act with his wife Roberta and later was the creator of Marcy exercise equipment.

While Les Stockton served his active duty in the Army and the Air Force, his wife Pudgy continued taking part in Beach activities, performing with Bruce Conner and other partners. Because of her unique role as a woman weightlifter, and because of her striking figure, she appeared in numerous magazines, and on the cover of forty-two publications throughout the world.

Patriotism, complete with brass bands, governed Muscle Beach during the war years and after. Labor Day and the Fourth of July always delivered big shows. A 1947 news clipping announced circus performers and strong men and "the fabulously popular and beautiful Pudgy Stockton."

When the war ended, a nation of young men had to pick up the loose ends of their lives and try to return to their version of normalcy. The same was true of Muscle Beach.

No longer kids, the Muscle Beach regulars tried to find their places in the world that was ever so slowly starting to accept them. Some of them like Bob Cockburn of the Four Aces and paratrooper Gene Smith didn't return. Others returned with missing limbs but still performed on the bars. At Muscle Beach, as always, all were welcome; everyone was accepted.

The fifties would see our coming of age. In the meantime, however, the war was over. It was 1945, time to head home, and for a while, at least, to be young.

Winning the first Mr. California competition was something I couldn't imagine until Vic Tanny helped make it a reality. I recently found measurements taken of me on August 23, 1941. Here's what the tape measure said when I was aged nineteen years, three months and weighed one hundred seventy-six pounds:

Height: 5'7½"
Chest: 47"
Waist: 30"
Thigh: 23"
Calf: 16¼"
Neck: 16½"
Biceps: 16¼"
Forearm: 14½"

CHAPTER FOUR

MUSCLES AND MOVIE STARS

"If all those people thought I was a movie star,
maybe I should try to get into the movies."
—Steve Reeves

Hollywood was much more accessible to the Muscle Beach population than it was to those in other parts of the state—at least that's how we felt. Almost everyone had a friend who worked for a studio or had appeared in a movie. For those of us used to performing for the thousands who lined the Beach, the silver screen didn't seem that far away. Show business was a natural next step.

◁ **This poster of Mae West adorned the Sahara Hotel and billboards throughout Las Vegas—that's how she looked when she had her act with the Muscle Beach guys.**

◁◁ **Mae West and her bodybuilders were represented by the William Morris Agency and broke records on the road.**

THE HOTEL THAT MADE LAS VEGAS
THE ENTERTAINMENT CAPITAL OF THE WORLD
HOTEL SAHARA

Roy Rogers was one of the first stars to hang out at the Beach. Roy hid from the crowds at Silent Leo's, the nickname for the Beach cafe that was owned by his pal Leo Khoury. Although far from an acrobat, Roy was in good shape from all the stunts he performed on his horse in the films he made. One day in the mid-thirties, he, Moe Most and circus performer Frankie Vincent, "the Mighty Mite," were watching three athletes perform a three-high on the platform. "Would you like to try that?" Frankie asked Roy. The cowboy was not at all intimidated and said yes. With Moe as understander and Vincent the number two man, the one-hundred-fifty-pound Rogers was suddenly on top—still wearing his boots. "I wish I had a picture of that one," Moe often lamented. "It was one of the highlights of the early days to know Roy Rogers was up there."

It was a natural for the Beach people to do stunts in films, so Russ Saunders,

The Knox Trio

Publicity photos for The Knox Trio, the kids I trained.

Glenn Sundby and his sister Dolores, of the Wayne-Marlin Trio, when they were appearing with the *Spike Jones Show*. Glenn is doing what we call a pistol grip here—showing only one visible finger of balance, while holding onto to an invisible pole.

Glenn Sundby, on top, with his sister, Dolores, and his partner, Wayne Long, around 1950, at the then-isolated Desert Inn.

Armand Tanny, Glenn Sundby, center, George Eiferman in Las Vegas.

Relna Brewer, Paula Unger and Joe Gold all worked as stunt doubles. Glenn Sundby and Wayne Long went on the road with their hand-balancing act. In order to earn money to open our Physical Services gym, Bruce Conner and I performed as far east as Chicago as "The Del Rios," sub-billed "Poetry in Motion." Bruce was top man, and I was on bottom. We worked throughout 1946 and most of 1947, when Dolly Walker (Robson) and I traveled as Del & Darnell, an adagio act in 1947 and most of 1948, until the gym was able to support itself.

Bruce and I opened the gym in August of 1948, and those matinees and one-night stands helped keep our doors open as we built up our

HOTEL SAHARA

clientele. Our gym was located up the street from Twentieth Century-Fox and many of our clients were film stars. The studio paid the monthly membership of fifteen to twenty dollars for some; others paid their own way.

Tyrone Power, Kirk Douglas, Robert Wagner, Mike Connors and Linda Christian worked out there. Stars were treated like everybody else in our gym. It wasn't unusual to see Evelyn Keyes, Bill Williams, and his wife Barbara Hale (better known as Della Street on *Perry Mason*) and Bing Crosby's wife Dixie Lee and their kids going about their workouts without fanfare or attention. On one day, we had all three major Tarzans—Lex Barker, Johnny Weissmuller and Buster Crabbe—visiting the gym at the same time.

Although few of them tried stunts the way Roy Rogers did, many Hollywood stars visited Muscle Beach, enjoying the performances along with the rest of the crowds. All but a few went unnoticed. Jane

◀◀ **Steve Reeves was without question the most beautiful person on the Beach full of very beautiful people. Here he shows off the form that, even to the regulars of Muscle Beach, made him look like a classic statue.**

▲ **Steve Reeves as Hercules in 1957.**

Russell always turned heads, but just sitting in the audience Jayne Mansfield got as many stares as the acrobats on the platform.

Even before his movie career, Steve Reeves turned more heads than the stars with big names. His was the most perfect body on Muscle Beach or any beach. During the fifties no one in Hollywood personified fitness and the ideal physique more than he did. When he got out of the Army in 1946, Reeves went to Los Angeles to visit a buddy. As he spent more time visiting the Beach, he encountered the familiar glances and the familiar questions greeted him. "Aren't you a movie star?" Again he thought about acting, more seriously this time, but not seriously enough to take action. On the GI Bill, he went to San Francisco, training to become a chiropractor, and he continued to work out. Then, in June 1947, he won the Mr. America title and along with it, offers to audition for film roles. The day he turned twenty-two, he received a contract with Cecil B. DeMille for the film *Samson and Delilah*. He still has the card he was given that admitted him to the set. He remembers walking into DeMille's office and seeing four huge pictures on the wall—Dorothy Lamour, Bob Hope, Alan Ladd—and Steve Reeves.

"You're my Samson," DeMille told him, "but you have to lose fifteen pounds."

Reeves lost five pounds, and his Muscle Beach friends told him that he was ruining his body. DeMille said, "Ten to go." He explained that although Reeves

◇ **With Steve Reeves below and Russ Saunders on top, those girls were in good hands. Reeves' shoulders were wide enough for three.**

was in ideal shape, the camera would make him look heavier, and DeMille wanted the audience to see exactly what he saw when he looked at Reeves.

Again his Muscle Beach pals reminded him that he'd won the Mr. America title. He didn't have to lose anything. But Reeves knew that he couldn't make a living at bodybuilding. He was frustrated and confused for good reason. When you're as lean and muscular as he was, you don't have that much to lose. After four months, when the weight didn't come off, DeMille released him from his seven-year contract. Instead, Victor Mature played the role of Samson. Reeves hadn't been finished by the violence of war, and he certainly wasn't finished by this setback. As his funds dwindled, he began to make plans for how he might earn a decent living. In 1948, he moved to Muscle Beach.

One day, as he walked along the Beach with fellow bodybuilder George Eiferman, they were approached by a tanned, blond woman. Joy Cretez asked if they would be interested in renting a room in her home for one dollar each per day. That sounded promising. Like others who had served, both were on the government's 52-20, twenty dollars per week for one year. Soon Joy had six Muscle Beach regulars living in Muscle House by the Sea.

"For me, those were the good old days, and I'll tell you why," Reeves said. "Eiferman and I were on the 52-20. I paid one dollar a night for the room, one dollar a day for food, and had six dollars left over at the end of the week."

Between occasional guest appearances on television, Steve Reeves worked odd jobs—everything from pumping gas to parking cars. Then came a break. He played a Tarzan-like character in *Kimbar–Lord of the Jungle*, a television pilot. Although the show never made it to television, it led to him being cast in another film, *Athena*, in 1954.

This time Italian film director Pietro Francisci, who was

▲ Steve Reeves poses on the rings at Muscle Beach.

◆ Reeves was always surrounded by female admirers.

desperately seeking an actor to play Hercules, spotted him. After seeing Reeves in *Athena*, the director's thirteen-year-old daughter said, "Daddy, I think you've found your Hercules." And he had.

Reeves went on to star in two Hercules films, both directed by Francisci, gaining fame and fortune in Italy. He made more than a dozen Italian films, mostly costume spectaculars in which he portrayed Hercules and other mythic heroes.

MAE'S MUSCLE BEACH MEN

In 1954, George Eiferman, Reeves' friend who had come to Los Angeles after winning the 1947 Mr. Philadelphia title, came down to the Beach and told his friends that Mae West was going to put together a nightclub act with nine different bodybuilders. Eiferman did his recruiting right there on the Beach.

A frequent participant at Muscle Beach from the moment he arrived on the west coast, Eiferman devoted his time to training seriously for bodybuilding contests—training that paid off. He won both the Mr. California and Mr. America titles in 1948, and was named Mr. Universe in 1962.

His recruiting for Mae West had come about after he met the aging sex symbol through their orthopedic surgeons. When she was considering starting up a new traveling night club act at the age of sixty-two, George convinced her to use bodybuilders in her show.

Although he'd never been on the stage, Joe Gold liked West and especially liked the two hundred fifty dollars a week he'd be paid, as well as the opportunity to meet chorus girls.

The original nine—all of them from Muscle Beach—were: Gold, Eiferman, Richard DuBois, who was the star, Harry Schwartz, Armand Tanny, Dom Juliano (a 1953 Mr. America finalist), Lester "Shifty" Shaefer, Irvin "Zabo" Kozewski (another Mr. America

When the industry publicity machines started working, how could they resist turning Reeves into a god?

Appearing in the Mae West show, here is Bert Goodrich, the first Mr. America, in 1939, before the AAU was involved. He was a tremendous track man, high jumper—a speedster. He also worked as a double for John Wayne and others. With Bert are, from the left, Joe Gold and Joe Baratta, Zabo Kozewski (who later bought Gold's gyms), and to the left of Bert, Steve Reeves and Lyle Fox who later became a personal trainer for Gregory Peck.

finalist for 1953), and Chuck Krauser, who later took the name Paul Novak. Dressed in elaborate togas, the bodybuilders represented different countries, and West's job was to pick one as the winner.

"It was a lot of fun," Eiferman said. "It was all new to us."

After ten months of his one-year commitment, Gold knew his future with Mae was dim, he said. "She caught me kissing this camera girl behind the stage, and she looked daggers at me. We were her boys, and if we wanted to do anything, it had to be with her."

Knowing she would fire him anyway, Gold decided to remain in Miami, where it was warm, but show officials convinced him to travel with the group for their Chicago appearance. Barely off of the plane and in his hotel room, Gold was then officially fired.

West couldn't have been too angry, because she hired Gold back for her 1956 show. Some of the new performers in this one included Mickey Hargitay, a Mr. Universe and the future husband of Jayne Mansfield.

Gold wasn't thrilled. According to his sexy boss, she was organizing the show

to help Lou Walters (father of Barbara Walters) boost up business at The Latin Quarter nightclubs. That's the reason West gave for cutting Gold's pay to one hundred twenty-five dollars per week. "This is no fun," Gold told Armand Tanny, "I'm going to quit."

"Think about it," Tanny said. "Maybe there's something we could do."

The weightlifters decided to strike for their regular pay of two hundred fifty

◊ **Armand Tanny was a weight-lifter, a wrestler and member of the original Mae West stage show.**

dollars, which they knew the dancers in West's show earned. When they arrived in New York, they made their demands.

"You'll never work again," West's representative shouted.

"We don't care," Gold and the others retaliated. "We're going back to Muscle Beach on the four o'clock plane."

By three that afternoon, Mae West's advisers had negotiated a deal.

One night, platinum-blond sex icon Jayne Mansfield attended West's show, and, when she was asked what she'd like to order, eyed Mickey Hargitay and replied, "The beefcake on the end." West insisted that the subsequent Mansfield-Hargitay dates were just public relations fiction.

When she discovered that Hargitay was picking up Mansfield every night after Mansfield's performance in the play *Will Success Spoil Rock Hunter*, she struck back. Gold remembers Hargitay coming down the stairs one night with "a big mouse over his eye." Paul Novak, Mae's lover, had punched him out, Gold said.

The show toured for three years breaking all records in attendance. Gold again joined West's show for the third time in 1959, but he grew tired of being on the road and longed to return to the Beach.

"And this time, I quit," Gold told his boss.

POSING FOR DALI

Russ Saunders made acrobatics an essential part of stunt work in films such as the *Three Musketeers*, where he doubled for Gene Kelly. He was tumbling at Muscle Beach when a director approached him and asked if he'd be interested in doing stunt work. He needed a tumbler for the background of *The Great Profile*, starring John Barrymore. Saunders got the job and many more to follow.

In *Saboteur*, he worked as a double for Robert Cummings, jumping, handcuffed off of a sixty-foot bridge and swimming a hundred yards in central California's Kern River. He also doubled for Alan Ladd in all of the star's films until he was drafted into the Army in 1942.

Saunders had more than five hundred films to his credit, including *Shane* and *Singing in the Rain*, his favorite. His greatest role, however, was as Jesus Christ, but not for a film.

In 1950, he had a one-of-a-kind interview at Warner Brothers and the role, as it turned out, was Jesus. The eccentric artist Salvador Dali had interviewed about six hundred people in Spain and New York. Then he got in touch with Jack

Warner and asked if he could help him find someone with the right build, someone who didn't look too muscular, someone like a sailor or a diver or a gymnast, he said.

"They called me through casting," Saunders said, "but instead of taking me to a stage where they interview people for stunt work, we went to Jack Warner's office."

He was introduced to Salvador Dali, complete with glass cane and wax moustache. The secretary gave him a pair of trunks and asked him to change in the men's room.

"I did that and I came out, and he asked me to raise my arm and turn around and do some mannerisms that he wanted," Saunders said. "I had no idea who he was. I didn't know how famous he was, and to go up to Jack Warner's office was unusual."

Dali nodded to Jack Warner, and the next morning at eight Saunders found himself in his own dressing room. Outside he saw a big cross on the ground and workers with pulleys and lights. Dali was sitting there supervising. It took four or five days to get the right angle, so that from Dali's point of view, Saunders was the crucified Christ going up to heaven. Saunders posed three weeks in preparation and another five weeks in Spain.

The *Christ of St. John* now hangs in Scotland's Glasgow Art Museum.

Salvador Dali and Russ Saunders.

Dali's renowned painting of Russ Saunders as Christ of St. John of the Cross that hangs in Glasgow's art museum.

TRAINER OF THE STARS

Native New Yorker Terry Robinson was born on Coney Island in 1916. In 1934, when he was eighteen, he won the Golden Gloves competition sponsored by the Police Athletic League. He weighed one hundred twenty-six pounds, and all he wanted to do was play football. He went to York, Pennsylvania, where John Grimek had already made a name for himself. Since he realized that Grimek had lifted weights to build his body and his fame, Robinson followed his lead. Before he graduated, he added ten pounds of muscle and was a halfback on his school football team.

▸ Cecil Charles took this photograph of Mr. New York Terry Robinson in 1949.

▾ Terry Robinson with his friend and client Mario Lanza.

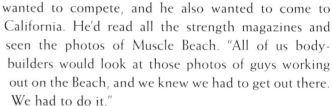

Robinson served in the Army and graduated from the noncommissioned officers' physical training school in Florida as a staff sergeant and was sent to Texas for further training. He was then assigned to the South Pacific to set up physical training and hand-to-hand combat classes. As the wounded started arriving at the hospitals, he set up physical rehabilitation for them. His Convalescent Training program focused on weight training and swimming as effective means of rehabilitation.

In 1946, he returned to New York. At that time in his life, Robinson wanted to compete, and he also wanted to come to California. He'd read all the strength magazines and seen the photos of Muscle Beach. "All of us bodybuilders would look at those photos of guys working out on the Beach, and we knew we had to get out there. We had to do it."

He was named Mr. New York in 1948, the same year he came to California. For a while he felt homesick, but eventually Robinson found his niche at Muscle Beach.

"It was family," he said. "I never had a day when I didn't have a friend." What he saw was a beach of acrobats, gymnasts, power lifters, bodybuilders and adagio acts, against a blanket of checkers and chess.

The wrestlers at the Beach, including "Baron" Michelle Leone, liked to play both. Every morning the Baron and Robinson would work out with

weights, but the Baron had chronic pain in his neck and shoulders. Robinson would give him stretches right there on the Beach. That was his ticket to the Muscle Beach crowd.

In order to work in California as a chiropractor, Robinson needed to take his state board examination and, in order to get his required hours, was working in a friend's office when he got a phone call that would change his life. Louis B. Mayer, legendary head of MGM Studios, had a stiff neck. Soon Robinson found himself in a limousine on his way to Bel Air.

"The Lord must have been looking down that day," he said. "When I touched him, he popped into place." Mayer was duly impressed. Two weeks later, Robinson was on salary, working with some of the top MGM stars: Clark Gable, Spencer Tracy, Robert Taylor and Tyrone Power. Robinson's first major challenge was Mario Lanza, who was twenty-five pounds overweight. Robinson accomplished the task of trimming Lanza down in three weeks, by taking him running at Muscle Beach. Robinson became Lanza's most trusted friend, so close, in fact, that when Lanza died suddenly at age thirty-eight, and his wife died a few months later, Robinson was named as a guardian of the four Lanza children, whom he raised.

Ultimately, movie stars—like the wrestlers and the circus people—were just another of the diverse elements that made up the Beach. The most interesting shows, the ones that attracted large audiences, were those we performed up on that platform. Although we didn't know it back then in the early fifties, those shows would soon be coming to an end.

CHAPTER FIVE

THE FINAL DAYS OF MUSCLE BEACH

"Muscle Beach was like a Roman holiday. We'll never have that again."
—George Eiferman, Mr. America 1948

After the war and into the fifties, many of us returned to Muscle Beach. A lot of servicemen who had been stationed in southern California during the war made good on their vows to come back and make it their new home. Overall, the Beach appeared to have weathered the war years pretty well. But the clock was already ticking; it was just that nobody could hear it. As the Beach itself began to slip away from us, what it and what we stood for was reflected in the way we lived our lives.

THE PAPA OF MUSCLE BEACH

In a small office in a wooden building there on the Beach, Moe Most helped with acrobatics and oversaw all activities. He also introduced numerous contests, including the first Miss Muscle Beach and Mr. Muscle Beach contests in 1947, as

◀ **Crowds were the reason for the Beach's success and also for its sudden closing.**

well as numerous tests of athletic ability. I remember winning on several occasions for being able to do the most handstand-press pushups. We did these on the low platform. It required going up into a handstand then bending the arms so that the chest was near the platform, then straightening the arms. It was sort of like a squat done with the arms instead of the legs, and I could do about twenty of them. Moe was creative with his challenges and serious in his commitment to the Beach. Indeed, "he was the papa at Muscle Beach," as Relna Brewer McRae fondly recalls.

Since the late thirties, weightlifting had been an activity at the Beach. I always worked out with the weightlifters when I wasn't on the platform, and others did the same. In the fifties, more people began lifting weights on the Beach. It became a popular event to watch and a few lobbied for weightlifters' rights. With Moe's help, the city agreed to give the weightlifters an L-shaped platform fifty yards west of our north/south platform. Eventually they formed the Muscle Beach Weightlifting Club. Although it was primarily an acrobats' beach, the weightlifters were welcome there.

WRESTLERS ON THE BEACH

Along with college athletes, acrobats and circus people, another group made their home on the Beach. Wrestlers doing their road work from Ocean Park to Muscle Beach found a comfortable, congenial place to relax after their run. It started with Gorgeous George, who originated gimmick wrestling in the late thirties. With his shoulder-length blond locks, he shocked and delighted audiences by throwing golden bobby pins, which he called "Georgie pins," to his fans.

Shaggy-haired wrestler Baron Leone was no glamour boy, but this top wrestler of the day loved to spend time at Muscle Beach. Around 1948, the Baron donated the first weights to the Beach. Until his generous act, Beach weightlifters had to bring their own metal. Looking like today's version of a street thug, he enjoyed his bad-guy image and used it to help promote his cause. Many young kids with

◁ **Another hard-working Sunday in the 1950s: Moe Most is on the bottom and I am second from the top. The stunt looks difficult, but it was relatively easy.**

▷ **The kids at the Beach were as involved in the mounts as the adults. The stunts definitely became a form of family entertainment.**

cigarettes in their hands had to deal with the Baron's wrath on the Beach. He'd walk up with his meanest wrestler face, yank the cigarette out of the kid's hand and deliver an anti-smoking admonition. He, like others who didn't smoke, were fighting the Hollywood image of smoking being sexy. The Baron, however, looked just threatening enough to make his message stick.

One of the greatest wrestlers who worked out at Muscle Beach as a kid, later appeared at San Francisco's Cow Palace before sell-out audiences. Jose Serapio Palomino Gomez Jr., became "Pepper" in grammar school, where classmates cheered him on in numerous events with shouts of "Pepe, Pepe, Pepper, Pepper, hot Pepper." A tumbler at Belvedere Junior High in east Los Angeles, he worked with my revered coach Harry Spencer. Although Gomez played baseball and ran track, his first goal was to play football. In order to do that, he had to build up his small frame.

At one hundred fifty-five pounds, he was already pretty fast, and he knew that weightlifting would make him stronger. He made his own weights out of cement and worked out in his backyard, and with increased strength, did make it into high school football.

Gomez joined the Navy, but when the war ended ten weeks later, he decided he'd had enough of the service. He enrolled in Los Angeles City College with the goal of becoming a coach. After almost two years, he got married and decided he needed to earn a living. While employed as a solicitor for a newspaper, he continued to work out passionately, often at the Beach.

Here's a time contest in the '50s, which isn't as easy as it looks. The females had to hold the males in a shoulder stand for three minutes.

◄ These kids were winners of the Junior Mr. Muscle Beach competition in the mid-1950s. At that time, a very big chest in the heavier weight division might be fifty inches. I was forty-eight inches at one hundred seventy-five pounds. Jack LaLanne was about the same, although he weighed less and probably had a smaller waist than I.

Around 1947, he and his younger friend Gene Meyers decided to work out at Vic Tanny's gym. Soon Gomez bench-pressed more than four hundred pounds and could squat with six hundred. He continued to build his body and did his best to ignore those who stereotyped him as musclebound. He was named Mr. Muscle Beach in 1950.

When he finally got his first offer of a match, Gomez said, "No, no, no," he recalls. "It scared the hell out of me." He eventually got over his stage fright and, in 1953, he traveled to Seattle and Portland and was named the Pacific Coast Junior Heavyweight Champion. He was also the heavyweight champion in Texas, where the primarily Hispanic audience screamed, "We love you, Pepper."

"I was a god in Texas and San Diego," he laughs. Always the underdog, Gomez won the collective heart of the audience when he'd pick up a three-hundred-pound opponent and spin him. One of his heroes was Jimmy Landis, a heavyweight

It was not unusual at Muscle Beach to see Mr. America/Mr. Universe George Eiferman playing his trumpet while pressing a weight with his other hand.

champion and a great wrestler. Gomez was wrestling in San Diego, when his idol came up to him and introduced himself.

"I want you to know that you remind me of me when I was a young man," he said. With those words, Pepper felt he had arrived. He still sounds as if he can't quite believe all that happened to him. "Can you imagine all of us working out at Vic Tanny's gym?"

SYMPHONY OF STRENGTH

Leo Stern, who was operating his eponymous gym in San Diego, had long enjoyed visiting Muscle Beach when he was in town for weightlifting competitions. Stern had a goal to stimulate interest in weightlifting using adagio, juggling and hand-balancing acts. At the Beach, he'd seen the odd assortment of types packing the boardwalk to watch the show, and perhaps unconsciously learning about physical fitness. "I wanted to stimulate the interest in weightlifting in conjunction with what was already acceptable," he said.

In 1947, after discovering that one of his members at the gym was a concert pianist, he came up with the idea of creating "Symphony of Strength." The variety show attracted its audience, much as Muscle Beach did, with jugglers, adagio, hand-balancing and other entertainment. In fact, Stern featured Muscle

◀ **The sign in the upper right corner of the photo is advertising Bruce Conner's and my first gym, Physical Services. This kid I'm balancing is as precious to me today as he was then. My son DeWayne knew to keep his arms and legs straight. Now an attorney, he and his wife Sandy are the parents of my granddaughter and three grandsons.**

Beach acts such as hand-balancers Walter and Roberta Marcyan and Pudgy and Les Stockton. At each show, Stern also introduced a weightlifter, such as 1945 Mr. America Clarence Ross or John Davis, who was the Olympic heavyweight lifting champion for fourteen years. Although the general public might not turn out for a weightlifting event, they would for a variety show. By watching these trained athletes perform, they also received the subtle message of fitness. "People understood the message of adagio and hand-balancing more than they did watching someone tossing iron around," Stern recalls.

"Symphony of Strength" ran from April of 1947 to 1962 in San Diego's Hoover High School auditorium, which held twelve hundred. Admission was two dollars a person, and standing-room-only was a common occurrence.

THE KIDS GROW UP

In April of 1949, Steve Reeves, George Eiferman and Pudgy and Les Stockton were invited by the Nuuana YMCA of Hawaii to help raise funds for the Y's national weightlifting club. They put on four different muscle shows on four different islands.

Tanned and wearing white, both Reeves and Pudgy Stockton were perfect specimens, her husband recalls. In his usual way, the fun-loving Eiferman decided that they should separate and let Pudgy and Reeves walk ahead. The others lingered behind twenty or thirty feet, listening to the comments of the people watching them.

"People were dumbfounded as they walked by," recalls Les Stockton, noting that people weren't used to seeing such incredible physiques on the beach.

After the Hawaii tour, Pudgy and Les Stockton remained active at Muscle Beach and opened their first gym in Los Angeles, next to Walter Marcyan's famed gym. Pudgy organized the first AAU-sanctioned weightlifting meet for women in 1946. But by 1953 they had three gyms and Pudgy was pregnant, so they had to limit their time at the Beach.

By 1949, when he was twenty-eight, Glenn Sundby had already become an entry in *Ripley's Believe It or Not!* for hand-walking down all eight hundred

His height and weight didn't hinder Wally Abro's balance and grace. Here, in the 1950s, he executes incredible balance on his wife Dodie's backbend. Wally is gone now, but this photograph is one of my favorites, because I so admire the positioning of both participants.

◁ **Mr. Muscle Beach Monte Wolford.**

◁▷ **Mickey Hargitay, husband-to-be of Mansfield, with Pudgy Stockton and Conner on the bottom.**

ninety-eight steps of the Washington Monument. He also earned a place in the book, *The Super Athletes: A Record of the Limits of Human Strength, Speed and Stamina*, by doing a planche (standing on hands at a forty-five degree angle, legs straight out behind) with a medicine ball between his legs and then a straight-leg press to handstand with three medicine balls between his legs.

Sundby did handstands all over the world, from the railing overlooking Niagara Falls to the Egyptian Pyramids. In Hawaii, he was the first to hold a handstand while riding a surfboard. In the late forties, Sundby was based in New York with the Wayne-Marlin Trio. About a year later, Glenn, his partner Wayne Long and his sister Dolores joined Spike Jones and his Musical Insanities show as hand balancers. When they appeared at the Biltmore Hotel in Los Angeles, they came down to Muscle Beach between acts. Dolores liked to play the jukeboxes in the beachfront cafes, especially big band music by Glenn Miller and Artie Shaw.

Their lives weren't all that different from the circus people and other professionals they met on the Beach. Traveling from town to town and coming back to the same train each night was hard work but it was offset by the good friends they made. The Sundbys' final tour with Spike Jones was to Australia in 1955 with a stopover in Hawaii.

George Eiferman had a successful career in bodybuilding, never losing his sense of humor. He often lifted weights with one hand and played the trumpet with the other. His first job was at our Conner/Zinkin gym in Los Angeles, where he taught bodybuilding in the late forties. He left the Beach and our gym in 1954 and opened Eiferman's Gym in Las Vegas, which he operated for fourteen years. The first of its kind in that city, it catered to many show people.

For fifteen years, Eiferman also worked for the National School Assembly Program touring schools all over the United States, some of them not even on the map. He often addressed ten thousand students in a single week. His goal was to convince students that they should be fit and that fitness would improve their lives.

"I was inspired by those young minds," he said. "I wanted them to know that they didn't have to settle for the bodies they were born with—they could improve and perfect them."

For years, Armand Tanny was a senior writer for the Weider publication

◀◀ In this photo by Barney Fry, George Wayne Long and Glenn Sundby do a double lever.

◀ Even with Russ Saunders and two women on top, Moe Most was the solid foundation of the Beach.

John Grimek holds Glenn Sundby in a hand-to-hand at a meeting in Chicago.

Muscle & Fitness. At seventy-nine, in 1998, he was still working out four times a week, looking twenty years younger than his actual age.

As we grew older, many of the regulars began spending more time away from the Beach. Some began raising families, and most of us became involved in our careers. Between 1946 and '50, I appeared on the cover of *York Strength and Health* twice, once in a classic pose by photographer Al Urban, who shot me in a pair of trunks with a sword.

In '52, I was contacted by two friends I had met in the Navy's physical instructor school. They wanted to open a gym in Fresno, then a small agricultural community in California's central valley. I suggested they spend some time with Bruce and me to see how demanding gym work was. "It's not show biz," I told them. "You'll be down there at seven and not closing until eleven at night."

They didn't listen, and the following year I got a call. They wanted to go on the road with their ice-skating/hand-balancing act. They offered me one-third of their business to run the gym for one year while they were gone. I loved the place, and they loved being away from it. I bought them out after a year. Within three years, I owned five gyms in Fresno and had my own television exercise show. My Muscle Beach days were over.

THE DESTRUCTION OF THE BEACH

Before long I started hearing from my southern California friends about problems cropping up at Muscle Beach. As I had experienced the Beach at its best before the war, it was difficult to imagine, let alone visualize, the rumors that its existence was in danger. A 1941 article in *Strength and Health* magazine stated, "Santa Monica takes no credit for the inception of the playground because it 'just grew' in the natural course of events." That was the general feeling—that the Beach just grew without the permission or the approval of the city.

In the '50s and '60s, Glenn Sundby published gymnastics magazines.

The city of Santa Monica had never figured out how to contend with the hordes of people who flocked to watch the acrobats every weekend. Cars trying to park created chaos on the roads. Crowds that ranged from two thousand to ten thousand thronged Muscle Beach on Sundays and brought chaos to the boardwalk as well. Its popularity had even inspired two Carmel residents, Ric Masten and Don Stevens, to write a 1958 song called "Muscle Beach." The tune was a parody about the "strong boys" of the ocean-front attraction site.

But by the late fifties, many Muscle Beach fans began to see the handwriting in the sand. Some believed the city wanted to take over the Beach to create more parking lots. Others blamed influential Ocean Park Pier business owners who didn't like the competition of free entertainment. Still others felt that the owners of the Surf Rider Hotel (where the Loew's Santa Monica Beach Hotel stands today) didn't think their guests would enjoy the unruly crowds. Whatever the reason, the city soon had a legitimate reason to disband the fun at Muscle Beach, or so it seemed.

In December 1958, five weightlifters who lived in a boardwalk apartment house near the Beach were reported partying at night with two underage girls and subsequently accused of statutory rape. "Officials Stirred as Sex Orgy Bared," read the headline in the legendary *Santa Monica Evening Outlook*. Although the five were arrested and charged with "morals offenses" the cases against the weightlifters were eventually dropped. The story was enough for the city to close down the Beach, pending further investigation.

For three months a heated debate ensued between the Santa Monica city council, Muscle Beach habitues and locals who were "embarrassed" and "disgusted" by the scandal. The council largely supported the idea of keeping the Beach closed for good, citing claims that in recent years it had become an attraction for "perverts" and "narcissistic parasites." Supporters argued that Muscle Beach had developed many outstanding athletes and had brought the city national attention, and that most of its users were "decent people."

◈ I couldn't resist including this publicity shot of the Wayne-Marlin Trio on the twenty-fifth floor of a Miami hotel. They would have done something like this at Muscle Beach, but there have never been hotels that tall in Santa Monica.

◈ That's me in the middle and John Grimek on the left, during this photo shoot at the Miramar Hotel, circa 1950. Our pal Sig Klein, from New York, had the first super gym in history.

The city also used the high cost of maintenance as an official reason for demolishing the Beach, stating that it cost about ten thousand dollars a year to operate and maintain. One night, shortly after the rape arrests were made, the city bulldozed the workout area and tore out the equipment. Even the equipment shack and personal weights, mats and other equipment disappeared.

A group that included Russ Saunders and Paula Boelsems met with a city councilman, but were told that the city council had not been contacted prior to the actions. The police department and city recreation department had ordered the bulldozer. The very day after the destruction of the Beach, dirt was brought in for the creation of parking lots, Boelsems said, although that plan was later abandoned.

Amid the controversy, Moe lost his job as Beach supervisor. "There was a lot of prejudice involved," he says of the time. "People didn't like weightlifters and thought there was something wrong with them. Athletes were not accepted like they are today."

In March 1959, the city council finally voted to reopen the Beach, adopting a pallid plan recommended by the city's recreation commission. The new terms mandated that the name "Muscle Beach" be discontinued; that weightlifting activities be dropped; that no public events be held without the approval of the recreation department; and that the area be supervised by a full-time director hired by the city.

The new Beach, outfitted with children's playground equipment and adult gymnastic equipment, was christened "Beach Park 4" and officially opened to the public in August.

Although the name and look of the Beach had changed, some of the faces stayed the same. Russ Saunders continued to bring his own teeter board, risley roll, trampoline, pedestal, mats and other equipment to the Beach, recalled Boelsems. In addition to the regulars who dared to return, Saunders worked, as he always had, with kids and even developed a group, the "Muscle Beach AcroBrats." However, the message from the city was clear: *not one handstand, not one pushup on the Beach.*

Russ and Paula traveled out of the area. As "Russell and Paulette," they performed a duo adagio and teeter board act all over the country and the world.

Moe, having no activities to direct, went to work in the studios as a carpenter on films such as the second version of *King Kong* and *9 to 5*.

The regulars, amateurs and professionals alike, were as disturbed by the

Here's Baron Leone with Beverly Jocher, Miss Muscle Beach of 1952. This guy was a "villain" in the imaginary world of wrestling, but he was a good friend to the kids of Muscle Beach. When Mario Lanza came to the Beach, usually in disguise, the singer liked to visit and speak his native Italian with one of the few there who knew his identity—Baron Leone.

MISS MUSCLE BEACH '52

▶ Tony Terlazzo, far right, was a weightlifter and an Olympian. Next to him is George Eiferman, then Armand Tanny and me. Bob McCuin is next to me (and no one can help me identify the sixth fellow). From about 1948 to 1951, we'd have weightlifting contests at our gym. The contestants were usually John Farbotnik, McCuin, Joe Weider and I. With hundred-pound dumbbells in each hand, we'd do dead-hand clings from the floor to our shoulders, never letting them touch the floor as we went down. I could do eight to ten at a time, and I'll leave it to my friends to tell you what they did.

destruction of Muscle Beach, as were those who came to watch. "It was a disappointment when we came back from Europe, and they had taken the platform away," Dodie Abro said. "That was such a nucleus. The Beach never regained the momentum that it had while that platform was there."

After establishing my Fresno gyms, I stopped by the Beach a few times when I was in the area. Instead of the second, north-to-south platform, I saw only a green patch of grass, about thirty by thirty feet. The patch of grass was supposed to replace our platform. It was called a recreation area, but other than a few kids doing handstands, there were no recreation activities, no performers, and of course, no audience. The platform was gone, and so was much of the power that had driven Muscle Beach.

By 1959, with Muscle Beach essentially destroyed, Joe Gold decided that he and other regulars should launch a Muscle Beach Weightlifting Gym, making it a non-profit corporation. It worked well, but they continually had to change its location to available buildings. Then, Gold came up with a better idea. If each of fifteen key people came up with one hundred fifty dollars, they could buy a building and give the gym a permanent home. Gold couldn't convince anyone to help.

"OK," he said, "I'll do it myself."

Like other early gym owners, he built the structure and all of his equipment himself. Gold's Gym opened in 1964 at 106 Pacific Avenue in Venice. Gold's approach was a heavy, hard, rugged workout for those who cared about serious bodybuilding. It was a no-mercy kind of gym, and he specialized in that approach.

He sold the gym in 1970, and its new owners developed the gym that bears Gold's name into an international chain of major renown. The real Gold returned for another tour as a merchant seaman. A few years later, he began World Gym, which he owns today and operates out of the main location in Venice.

The Muscle Beach phenomenon helped spread the message of fitness across the nation. "The Muscle Beach guys trained naturally, and they followed the laws of life and health," explains Vic Boff, founder of the Association of Oldetime Barbell & Strongmen based in Cape Coral, Florida. "To them the care of the body was a sacred responsibility."

Indeed, we all understood that responsibility, if not literally, then intuitively. In the forties and fifties, casual interest in nutrition, physical fitness and obtaining one's best potential physical shape were not popular subjects to the mainstream public. As Steve Reeves, who turned seventy-three in 1999, recalls. "On

Muscle Beach, there were physical culturists who were discussing such subjects as the benefits of goat's milk, yogurt and certain exercises." Although it may sound commonplace today, in the early days of Muscle Beach, alternative nutrition was revolutionary thinking, and it contributed to the Beach's appeal.

At one time, we were social outlaws because we believed that people had to move, even if they were ill or had physical disabilities. Today, weight rooms are common parts of hospitals. Exercise and nutrition are recognized for their contributions to long life and overall health. It's come full circle. Muscle Beach, as we knew it, may be gone, but the Muscle Beach attitude is not. Those of us who were around in the early days feel vindicated—happy to be alive and still flexing our muscles.

‖⚊‖

EPILOGUE

I hope the tales, tall and short, I've shared in this book about the original Muscle Beach help to illuminate what was a vital era in southern California history. To those of us there throughout the thirties, forties and fifties, it was a place that lived and breathed its own spirit into all of us. Now, some forty years after the Muscle Beach I knew closed, it appears that the spirit of Muscle Beach is perhaps being reincarnated—if that's possible. The city of Santa Monica has reopened the Beach once again south of the Santa Monica Pier, just a little over three hundred yards from where it once existed. As part of the city's Beach Improvement Group (BIG) Project, a new Ocean Front Walk will curve around the area of an expanded Muscle Beach, placing benches along the pedestrian path. Some of the older existing equipment has been repaired and stands proudly next to new equipment. Can it ever be the same again? No. But maybe it will generate a new kind of enthusiasm, and spread a new message.

A VIEW OF THE BEACH

Talk to anyone from Muscle Beach and sooner or later, you'll hear a term that indeed describes the spirit of the place. The word is "pioneering," and when used by the Muscle Beach crowd, its grammatical shortcomings are overshadowed by what it means to these people. By refusing to accept the bodies with which we were born, we were pioneering for a way of life that had yet to be recognized. Proactive

◄ **This is the way I remember those invincible summers at Muscle Beach.**

and far from passive, we weren't just pioneers, we were actively, passionately pioneering. And most of us have lived to see our work rewarded as the physical fitness movement swept this country.

In a world of doubters, our pioneering spirit helped unify us. Many of us thought of the Beach as a second home, and our friends there were as close as family. Muscle Beach was a place where we found others who believed as we did. Strong women in a world ruled by men, weightlifters fighting stereotypes, health advocates dismissed as crackpots. All of us, myself included, found safety, acceptance and fun at Muscle Beach.

We were kids breaking with the past and not always by choice. Steve Reeves, Glenn and Dolores Sundby and Bruce Conner had to deal with the death of a parent while barely more than children themselves. I lost my father at a young age, which necessitated my dropping out of high school to help support my mother.

The war prematurely forced the realities of life on John Kornoff, Joe Gold and the rest of us. We were beginning to realize that we would be living in a different world from the one in which we were raised. In some ways, we were as homeless as the circus people in whose footsteps some of us followed when we took our own acts on the road.

Like family, we stayed together, despite the miles between us, bonded for life. Pudgy Stockton and Relna Brewer McRae are still as close as sisters. Les Stockton wrote his "Rhymed Muscle Beach Memoir" for Bruce Conner on the occasion of Bruce's eightieth birthday. Glenn Sundby used his own money to record, through newsletters, the various accomplishments of the Muscle Beach crowd. In 1998, Paula Boelsems cared for two of her Muscle Beach friends through serious illnesses.

AN INVINCIBLE SUMMER

As in all families, time has taken its toll. John Grimek, the inspiration for most of the Muscle Beach athletes, died suddenly on November 20, 1998, at his home in York, Pennsylvania.

What remains of the Beach exists only in the memories of those who celebrated their youth there. "There was no place like it in the whole world," Sundby says of Muscle Beach. "There was a camaraderie that I could never find again."

Traveling acrobat/dancer Dodie Abro said that "the welcome warmth" she and husband Wally felt at the Beach made her look forward to seeing the group each time she was in town. "There was an element of competition, but yet it was in such a friendly way and a helpful way that you kind of bounced off of one another's ideas and helped one another," Abro said.

Although we were changing the course of fitness in the country, it felt much simpler than that. Our Beach was a place of fun and acceptance, a place that was "like family," especially to those who had less than that elsewhere. At Muscle Beach, you needed only to show up to be part of that family of kids where you were not John Kornoff, but JK, not Irving but Mousey or Whitey or Pudgy, or Moe or Zink.

Muscle Beach was about people ahead of their time—young people separated, in some way from their pasts and their parents. Those parents had been beaten into submission, but after the Great Depression, many of the kids muscled up.

"Everybody was stimulated, motivated and thrilled," LaLanne said. "You'd see these guys, and that gave you the incentive. Pride and discipline. That's what kids don't have today. These kids had something to look forward to."

Even if the Beach had not been closed, its fascination would have faded. Entertainment became more readily available. Times and values changed rapidly. We who frequented the Beach went from a paradise that lacked pollution and drugs into what we now know as the real world. We took a little bit of Muscle Beach into that world with us. Those values we shared—our willingness, at a young age, to differ and disagree with what was then considered normal—has kept most of us connected and close.

"I was down there until the day I couldn't walk," Joe Gold said. "I still go down there now and then to see the old cronies. The most important thing we had at Muscle Beach was the friendships."

If I could tell one story to illustrate the feelings of those days long ago, it would be this one. As I sat in a convertible talking with my friend John Farbotnik, a former Mr. America, some friends of his approached, and we all shook hands. One was a German who spoke no English, and I didn't speak his language. Yet, when we shook hands, I could tell by his grip that he was an acrobat, and I guess he could tell the same about me. Without saying a word, I put my hands in position. He grasped them, and as I still sat in the car, he went into first a regular and then a one-arm handstand before dismounting. We shook hands again, and he walked away.

That was our hello and goodbye, spoken with a smile, a handshake and the universal language of acrobatics.

Ultimately, the real story of Muscle Beach is not about a place but about an attitude and about people like Joe Gold, who has trained some of the world's best athletes, and like Terry Robinson, who works as morning manager at Sports Club L.A., a very trendy health club in west Los Angeles. Terry is up each morning by three-thirty. The trainers say to the members, "See that guy with the gray hair? Can you believe it—he's eighty-two years old."

"And now I'm their inspiration," Robinson acknowledges.

Inspiration. That's a fine word, especially considering that we didn't start out inspiring anyone except each other.

What might have felt like fun and looked like entertainment was the beginning of a fitness education for an uninformed nation. As the war stressed our minds and our bodies, that nation took a long, serious look at fitness. After the war, those who'd never known how good they could look and feel after running miles a day on a regular basis, wanted to maintain that positive feeling. Before long, what we believed and practiced at Muscle Beach started sounding less and less crazy.

Yet without Leo Stern, without Relna Brewer, Joe Gold, Pudgy Stockton, Moe Most, Steve Reeves, Johnny Kornoff and all of the others whose lives you've followed in this book, Muscle Beach would have been a different place, and we might have had to wait a lot longer to see fitness accepted. Not everyone on Muscle Beach in those early days was a fitness pioneer. A few just liked the sun and the sights, and that was all right, as well. Still, it's easy to be positive and upbeat when you're young. None of us (except LaLanne, of course) is young anymore. It's tougher to practice when we're forced to look unflinchingly at big numbers like eighty and ninety. We couldn't do that if we weren't who we are, and the Beach played a big part in helping us discover that.

This place that was called a paradise, a circus, a Camelot, a family, was all of those to most of us. All the sensations and experiences of the Beach remain within us as we face the rest of our lives. They may be as much or even more important than what we accomplished in those days. For in the end, we—and not that piece of sand—are Muscle Beach. Our legacy is greater than anything that remains there.

In the beginning, the Beach may have been what made the people, but ultimately, always, it was the people who made the Beach.

ACKNOWLEDGMENTS

Our thanks to Angel City Press publishers Scott McAuley and Paddy Calistro for agreeing to take on this project, and for their generosity and grace throughout the process. Thanks also to Relna McRae and her daughter, Lynne Kuhn, who reviewed the manuscript in progress and clarified the story of Muscle Beach's origins. No one could have a more talented administrative back-up team than Betty Curry and Anne Black, who came through on numerous occasions and usually after quitting time. Art directors Susan Anson and Maritta Tapanainen and copy editor Jane Centofante went above and beyond to help make this the book we visualized. We are grateful to the many photographers for whom the Muscle Beach stars posed in exchange for photos, and especially to the late Cecil Charles, whose early photos helped spread the magic of Muscle Beach to the rest of the world. We would also like to acknowledge Cecil's widow, Aileen, along with Glenn Sundby, who contributed historical information and hundreds of photographs, Paula Boelsems, who gave numerous photographs and who made herself available for many hurried phone calls, and Angela Grimek, Vic Boff, Norma Goodrich, and Bill Pearl for their assistance. Thanks, too, to Fred Basten for his photo of the Beach and Pier. Special thanks to Harold's family: May they carry the legacy of Muscle Beach into the future. And thanks to Bonnie's family, Ted, Jennifer and Matt Badasci, for their unconditional support while Bonnie was in "book mode." Finally, to those who shared their memories while being interviewed for this book, we are most grateful—for they were and always will be the real Muscle Beach: Dodie Abro, Paula Boelsems, Paul Brewer, Relna Brewer McRae, Don Brown, Irving "Mousey" Cohen, Bruce Conner, Dolores Dersch Foster, George Eiferman, Joe Gold, Pepper Gomez, John Grimek, Arnie Klein, Johnny Kornoff, Jack LaLanne, Deforrest "Moe" Most, Steve Reeves, Terry Robinson, Russ Saunders, Jim Starkey, Kay Starkey, Leo Stern, Les Stockton, Pudgy Stockton, Glenn "Whitey" Sundby, and Armand Tanny.